Online Resources

Congratulations! You now have access to practical templates of the Personal Finance concepts that you will learn in this book. These downloadable templates will help you implement your learnings in the real world and give you an in-depth understanding of the concepts. The templates include:

1. Income and Expense Statement

2. Balance Sheet

3. Budget Planner

To access the templates, follow the steps below:

1. Go to **www.vibrantpublishers.com**

2. Click on the **'Online Resources'** option on the Home Page

3. Login by entering your account details (or create an account if you don't have one)

4. Go to the Self-Learning Management series section on the Online Resources page

5. Click the **'Personal Finance Essentials You Always Wanted To Know'** link and access the templates.

Happy self-learning!

This page is intentionally left blank

SELF-LEARNING MANAGEMENT SERIES

PERSONAL FINANCE ESSENTIALS

YOU ALWAYS WANTED TO KNOW

An introduction to managing your personal finances better

ANKUR MITHAL

Personal Finance Essentials You Always Wanted To Know

First Edition

Paperback ISBN 10: 1-63651-184-8
Paperback ISBN 13: 978-1-63651-184-9

Ebook ISBN 10: 1-63651-185-6
Ebook ISBN 13: 978-1-63651-185-6

Hardback ISBN 10: 1-63651-186-4
Hardback ISBN 13: 978-1-63651-186-3

Library of Congress Control Number: 2023942250

This publication is designed to provide accurate and authoritative information in regard to the subject matter covered. The Author has made every effort in the preparation of this book to ensure the accuracy of the information. However, information in this book is sold without warranty either expressed or implied. The Author or the Publisher will not be liable for any damages caused or alleged to be caused either directly or indirectly by this book.

Vibrant Publishers books are available at special quantity discount for sales promotions, or for use in corporate training programs. For more information please write to bulkorders@vibrantpublishers.com

Please email feedback / corrections (technical, grammatical or spelling) to spellerrors@vibrantpublishers.com

To access the complete catalogue of Vibrant Publishers, visit www.vibrantpublishers.com

SELF-LEARNING MANAGEMENT SERIES

TITLE	PAPERBACK* ISBN

ACCOUNTING, FINANCE & ECONOMICS

COST ACCOUNTING AND MANAGEMENT ESSENTIALS	9781636511030
FINANCIAL ACCOUNTING ESSENTIALS	9781636510972
FINANCIAL MANAGEMENT ESSENTIALS	9781636511009
MACROECONOMICS ESSENTIALS	9781636511818
MICROECONOMICS ESSENTIALS	9781636511153
PERSONAL FINANCE ESSENTIALS	9781636511849

ENTREPRENEURSHIP & STRATEGY

BUSINESS PLAN ESSENTIALS	9781636511214
BUSINESS STRATEGY ESSENTIALS	9781949395778
ENTREPRENEURSHIP ESSENTIALS	9781636511603

GENERAL MANAGEMENT

BUSINESS LAW ESSENTIALS	9781636511702
DECISION MAKING ESSENTIALS	9781636510026
LEADERSHIP ESSENTIALS	9781636510316
PRINCIPLES OF MANAGEMENT ESSENTIALS	9781636511542
TIME MANAGEMENT ESSENTIALS	9781636511665

*Also available in Hardback & Ebook formats

SELF-LEARNING MANAGEMENT SERIES

TITLE	PAPERBACK* ISBN

HUMAN RESOURCE MANAGEMENT

DIVERSITY IN THE WORKPLACE ESSENTIALS	9781636511122
HR ANALYTICS ESSENTIALS	9781636510347
HUMAN RESOURCE MANAGEMENT ESSENTIALS	9781949395839
ORGANIZATIONAL BEHAVIOR ESSENTIALS	9781636510378
ORGANIZATIONAL DEVELOPMENT ESSENTIALS	9781636511481

MARKETING & SALES MANAGEMENT

DIGITAL MARKETING ESSENTIALS	9781949395747
MARKETING MANAGEMENT ESSENTIALS	9781636511788
SALES MANAGEMENT ESSENTIALS	9781636510743
SERVICES MARKETING ESSENTIALS	9781636511733

OPERATIONS & PROJECT MANAGEMENT

AGILE ESSENTIALS	9781636510057
OPERATIONS & SUPPLY CHAIN MANAGEMENT ESSENTIALS	9781949395242
PROJECT MANAGEMENT ESSENTIALS	9781636510712
STAKEHOLDER ENGAGEMENT ESSENTIALS	9781636511511

*Also available in Hardback & Ebook formats

About the Author

 **Ankur Mithal** is a widely experienced author and business professional. His 15 years of experience with Standard Chartered Bank lent him extensive financial knowledge which he has poured into this book. He delivered roles in sales where he guided clients in their purchase of financial products/services, investing, and borrowing; as well as project management and operations where he led multiple cross-border multicultural teams. He was also involved in setting up the bank's first Priority Banking Center in India.

In addition to banking and finance, he has worked closely with the BPO and E-learning industries. His other published works include:

1. Some Method Some Madness, Managing BPO in India – a guide to the BPO industry

2. What Happens in Office, Stays in Office – a collection of satirical stories about office life

3. Organizational Development Essentials You Always Wanted To Know – A book for young professionals on the subject of Organizational Development

Ankur operates as a business consultant and freelance writer, apart from working on his own writing projects.

Other Contributors

We would like to thank our editor, Kalpesh Ashar for his contribution to making this book the best version possible. Kalpesh is a management consultant and corporate trainer holding an MBA (Dean's Award Winner) from SPJIMR, one of Asia's top business schools, and an engineering degree with honors in electronics. He has over 24 years of experience in large organizations and start-ups in Asia, USA, and Europe. Kalpesh has worked in several project management roles, including senior project manager, delivery manager, and program manager. He is passionate about writing on management subjects. His techno-business background gives him a unique position to write on management topics that are easy to understand for non-MBA graduates. His books are authored in simple language without unnecessary use of management jargon.

What experts say about this book!

Personal Finance Essentials You Always Wanted To Know is an introductory source for those wanting to learn basic personal finance concepts. I often find that personal finance books either over-complicate or over-promise the benefits to the reader. However, this work does an effective job of bridging the gap between practice and theory by only emphasizing the essential components of both. By exposing the reader to a broad range of important concepts, this book is an appropriate starting point for those needing a framework to understand the importance and application of personal finance concepts within their own life.

**– James Meersman, Assistant Professor,
Juniata College**

Ankur Mithal's *Personal Finance Essentials You Always Wanted to Know* provides a thorough overview of personal finance topics for the novice and others who want to backfill holes in their knowledge.

I'm pretty savvy on many of the topics discussed in this book, but still, Mithal managed to surprise me with facts I didn't know. The book is written in layperson language, making it easy to understand and consume. I didn't have to look up words or memorize ideas to figure out what Mithal was saying. He kept it so simple that each topic organically grew from prior ones. Each chapter includes a chapter summary and a quick quiz to review essential topics and remind readers of the important elements. I'm not a fan of quizzes but in this case, it serves the serious student well to confirm their knowledge base for the upcoming chapters.

Overall, this is recommended to those with an interest in money and personal finance who might consider these topics too complicated.

**– Jacqui M, Author and Adjunct Professor,
California State University and University of California San Diego**

What experts say about this book!

Personal Finance Essentials You Always Wanted To Know is a comprehensive guide that provides readers with a solid foundation in the realm of personal finance. The book's structure is well thought out, making it accessible to individuals at various stages of their financial journey, from beginners to seasoned practitioners.

What sets this book apart is its ability to break down the often intimidating world of taxes, helping readers understand the distinctions between different tax types and their respective responsibilities. One of the book's highlights is its treatment of retirement planning, a subject that holds immense significance for many readers. Each chapter's conclusion is marked by a well-crafted summary that elegantly ties together the key points discussed, serving as a valuable reference for readers. Additionally, the inclusion of quizzes at the end of each chapter enhances the learning experience, ensuring that readers absorb and retain the material effectively.

In sum, this book is a must-read for anyone seeking to navigate the complex world of personal finance. Written by an experienced professional, it caters to a broad audience, making it equally beneficial for those taking their first steps in financial planning and those looking to refine their existing knowledge and skills.

– Arkadiusz Mironko, Associate Professor of Management and Entrepreneurship, Indiana University East

Table of Contents

8   Insurance   147

9   Taxation   173

10   Retirement Planning   185

This page is intentionally left blank

Preface

Though it may have come into being as a means to an end, of facilitating the exchange of goods and services between human beings, money has grown in importance and today requires management for its own sake.

The accumulation, preservation, and growth of money is a need for every individual. The various streams of knowledge that come together to enable individuals and households to manage money is known as personal finance.

Personal finance is an all-encompassing term that covers how a person or household marshals the resources that can be expressed in the form of money that is available to them. It encompasses income and expenditure, budgeting, insurance, banking, investing, savings, tax planning, retirement, and many other aspects connected with money and finance.

With the options and opportunities for earning and spending, buying and selling, investing, and saving having multiplied, it has become more important than ever before for individuals to be financially knowledgeable so that they can make decisions related to personal finance in a manner that delivers long-term benefits.

This book seeks to educate common people on the basics of personal finance and make them aware of the possibilities.

It is for everyone interested in knowing a little more about personal finance.

This page is intentionally left blank

Introduction to the book

It is difficult to imagine a world without money. Money is commonly used as a medium of exchange. When we buy a car, we pay for it in money. When we eat at a restaurant, we pay for it in money. We can pay in the form of paper currency, or through one of the many digital modes in which it is held. Money is also used as a store of value. I can choose to retain the money I have and use it for buying goods and services at a later date.

As human beings, we understand the relevance of money in every sphere. The management of money is covered by the subject of personal finance which is what this book deals with. It is one subject that touches the life of every individual. Hence, it is important that every individual has a basic knowledge of the subject so that he/she can manage personal finances in a manner most suitable to his/her situation and goals in life.

Personal finance covers a wide range of areas, apart from the obvious ones like saving and investing money. An understanding of personal finance should cover:

- Personal finance basics – such as income and expense, asset and liability, and financial statements

- Budgeting and making a financial plan for the future

- Banking – types of accounts and facilities

- Investment choices and fundamentals of investing

- Borrowing – types of credit, credit risk, credit score

- Home – buy or rent decision, mortgage loans

- Insurance – life, car, home, health

- Taxation – income, property, sales, etc.

- Retirement and estate planning

This book addresses all these subjects intending to give an understanding of each to the reader. By the end of this book, one will be able to answer all questions related to these subjects.

With this understanding, readers should be equipped to ask the right questions and get the answers they need to reach optimum solutions that best meet their needs. This book will equip readers to know about the tools that exist through which they can manage personal finances better.

How to use this book?

The book is designed to provide an understanding of the basics of personal finance, including an overview of the various areas included in the scope. It also seeks to create an understanding of how deeply intertwined personal finance is with our lives.

The book is, perhaps, best negotiated with an open mind regarding the possibilities and the paths it could lead to and the various options and opportunities that may be available as we navigate the pathways of personal finance.

It should not be seen as providing the final answer to a specific situation. In fact, many of the parts that constitute personal finance keep changing. Interest rates go up and down. Taxation slabs change. Environmental factors such as inflation and FED policies also exert pressure for change. Specific, final answers should be arrived at by seeking current information with or without the help of specialists. The purpose of this book is to create a perspective and overview that enables readers to appreciate the many choices and options that are available to them.

This page is intentionally left blank

Who can benefit from this book?

The book is primarily designed to be of use to the common man who needs to make personal finance decisions almost on a daily basis but neither has background or training on the subject, nor any immediate support.

It creates a perspective for the common man, and woman, so that there is an appreciation of the options as well as an implication of decisions they take today in the longer run.

While creating this perspective, the book also seeks to dispel the fog of complexity that shrouds the subject of personal finance, creating hurdles in the path of the common man engaging with it and understanding it.

Practitioners might also wish to use the book as a point of reference and focus on the subject that is their area of work, be it insurance, mortgage loans, or retirement consulting. The book should help refresh and reset their perspective.

Of course, anyone with a desire to know more about the subject would benefit from reading this book as well.

This page is intentionally left blank

Chapter 1

Introduction to Personal Finance

This chapter introduces the concept of personal finance, the common thread that runs through many disparate parts of our lives. While it has traditionally been a means to achieving an end, such as buying food or renting a house, today finance has become an end in itself. "Let us take care of the finances, the rest will fall in place" seems to be the thinking today. Personal finance is similar to and closely intertwined with the concept of money.

Key learning objectives of this chapter include the reader's understanding of the following:

- Introduction to finance
- What is money
- The origin of money

- The value of money
- Currency and Foreign currency

1.1 Introduction to Finance

Taking a loan to buy a house is an example of a financial transaction. As is investing money in government bonds. Or, buying a coffee for cash at the streetside store.

Finance is an all-encompassing term, perhaps best described through examples, as done above. It is how any organization or person marshals the resources that can be expressed in the form of money, that are available to them.

According to the Corporate Finance Institute (CFI), "Finance is defined as the management of money and includes activities such as investing, borrowing, lending, budgeting, saving, and forecasting."[1]

1.2 What is Money?

Many times, finance tends to be used interchangeably with money. While they are closely related, they are not the same. Moreover, finance is expressed and quantified in the

---

1. "Finance Definition,"Wealth Management, Corporate Finance Institute, last modified June 15, 2023, https://corporatefinanceinstitute.com/resources/wealth-management/what-is-finance-definition/

form of money, and hence, in order to understand finance, an understanding of money is necessary.

As human beings, we understand the relevance of money in every sphere. In the modern world, it is used as a medium of exchange for buying and selling whatever we want. If we want to buy a house, we have to pay money for it. If we want to sell a car, we will receive money for it. Money is also a store of value, the unit in which accounting is done, and the standard for deferred transactions.

Money can be held in two primary forms:

1. **Physical cash** – When I buy fruits at the local grocery, I can pay for it in cash.

2. **Money in an account** – Money can be held in an account with an institution, known as a bank, that is authorized to do so. When I shop online, I can pay for the purchase from the balance in my account at the bank.

The rapid spread of telecommunication technology has also given rise to digital wallets, usually linked to mobile phones, in which money can be held. Regulations governing money held in non-bank wallets are evolving.

1.3 History of Money

The use of money has evolved over time. The earliest humans, self-sufficient in the groups they lived in, relied on division of labor as a means of equity and distribution. There was no need for any "commercial" transactions as the group was self-sufficient.

As society developed, humans started coming into contact with each other, and the need for transactions was felt. Systems such as barter, which involved exchanging something for another thing, are believed to have come into being almost 100,000 years ago. Of course, accurate determination of the equivalence of goods exchanged was not possible.

This gave way to the use of commodity money, which could standardize measurement in one common unit, regardless of what it was. A shekel, a unit of weight equivalent to around 160 barley grains, was adopted by Mesopotamian societies. In some other parts of the world, cowry shells gained currency as a medium of exchange.

The use of relatively modern units of exchange, in the form of gold and silver coins that possessed an intrinsic value for which they could be exchanged is dated to around 600 BC.

The Song dynasty of China is believed to be the first to have used banknotes as a medium of exchange around the seventh century. In being money that represented value, without possessing any intrinsic value of its own, the banknote system that has survived till today is perhaps more similar to the commodity money referred to earlier, than the gold and silver coins-based system which was based on intrinsic value.

The concept of paper money then traveled to Europe with most European powers issuing currency notes by the 18th century. Soon after, a gold-based standard came into being which required issuing governments to maintain gold reserves to back the currency issued, in order to avoid reckless issuance.

By the seventh decade of the 20th century, governments, led by the US, had started unshackling currency issuance from the gold-based standard, lending to it a certain purity in the form of "fiat" money that derives its value from social convention and widespread acceptance than any specific peg.

1.4 The Value of Money

The gold standard was adopted as the monetary system at the Bretton Woods conference in 1932. Paper notes issued by the central bank were backed by, and convertible into, quantities of physical gold held by the issuer. Thus, the use of gold as the medium of exchange gave way to paper currency which made it easier to be carried and traded with.

The Bretton Woods conference held after World War II to determine an economic system led to the adoption of fiat currencies that were linked to one common currency, the US dollar. The US dollar, in turn, was fixed to gold at the rate of $35 an ounce. Thus, not much changed.

When the US government suspended the convertibility of the US dollar to gold, the backing came unstuck. This move of the US government was then followed by other countries. In time, most currencies became unbacked by anything other than the issuing government's fiat making it legal tender.

When the concept of money was evolving, there was a phase when it held intrinsic value, such as in the form of gold coins that could be exchanged for goods and services equivalent in value.

However, in the modern world, the prevalence is of unbacked fiat money that derives its value because a regulatory entity has declared it to be so. A $20 bill has a value equivalent to $20 because the government has decided it to be the legal tender equivalent to $20 in value and the same has been accepted through popular use and social convention.

1.5 Currency/Foreign Currency

Money being a legislated entity, its value is accepted as defined within the governance boundaries of the authority defining it, which is national governments. Thus, the ability of a $20 bill to buy goods and services worth $20 is relevant only within the United States of America.

If one goes from the US to another country, say Germany, US dollars are of no use as the fiat currency used is different; it is the Euro. To buy anything in Germany, the traveler would need to have money in the form of Euros.

The other challenge that arises is that of equivalence.

USD 1 is not equivalent to EUR 1. It could be more or it could be less. The price of one currency in relation to another is known as the exchange rate. Most major currencies like the US dollar, Japanese, Yen and Euro are free-floating and their exchange value is determined based on supply and demand.

A can of Coke costing $1 in the US and 10,000 rupiah in Indonesia does not mean it is 10,000 times more expensive in Indonesia. All it means is that 1 US dollar may be close in value to 10,000 Indonesian rupiahs. Of course, there will be other factors that influence price too, but the exchange rate is probably the major reason in this case.

Most of us will probably encounter exchange rates at the airport when we travel to another country. Foreign exchange traders will have counters at airports to ensure that people traveling to another country that uses a different currency can exchange their dollars for the destination currency so that they can get around.

This is an abbreviated version of a board you might see at the airport foreign exchange counter:

Table 1.1	Sample currency exchange rates		
Currency	**Sign**	**Buy**	**Sell**
Euro	EUR	0.9418	0.9618
Japanese Yen	JPY	136.71	139.71
Indian Rupee	INR	82.59	84.59
Australian Dollar	AUD	1.4851	1.5151

- All prices equivalent to $1
- Figures used only for illustration

Why are there two rates? If you go from the US to India, you will need Indian rupees (₹) in exchange for your US dollars. When you return from India, you might wish to exchange the remaining foreign currency back to your own so that you can use it. If you exchange $100 while going, you will receive ₹8,259.

Assuming you return without spending anything, and assuming the rates have not moved, how many dollars will you get back? You now have ₹8,259 with you. The rate that is applicable when you return them will be 84.59. You sell ₹84.59 and receive $1. If ₹84.59 gets you $1, how many dollars will ₹8,259 fetch you? 8,259/84.59 = $97.63. This is because now the selling rate is applicable. This also represents the margin of the traders who incur cost and effort in offering this service and take a risk of exchange fluctuation.

The exchange rate itself does not indicate the relative wealth or poverty of the two nations.

1.6 Personal Finance, Corporate Finance, and Public Finance

1.6.1 Personal finance

It deals with the management of money by individuals and households. It encompasses income and expenditure, budgeting, insurance, banking, investing, savings, tax planning, retirement, and many other aspects connected with money and finance. With the options and opportunities for earning and spending, buying and selling, investing, and saving having multiplied, it has become more important than ever for individuals to be financially knowledgeable so that they are able to make decisions related to personal finance in a manner that delivers long-term benefits.

1.6.2 Business finance

Also known as corporate finance, this area of finance deals with the financial activities of businesses and organizations. It seeks to ensure that money is available for activities, it is put to the most optimum use, and external responsibilities such as taxation and filing of returns are carried out as required. Equity or debt, pricing, income distribution, mergers, and acquisitions are some noteworthy business finance activities.

1.6.3 Public finance

The role of government in the economy is covered in the study of public finance. Like individuals, households, and corporations, the government also has the responsibility of managing its finances in an optimal manner. The taxes it collects need to be distributed to the areas that need the money. The government's financial objective has to be to promote financial security, economic stability, and wealth-creation among the people and corporations. In many cases, governments can also raise money through other means such as sovereign bonds.

1.7 Factors That Affect Personal Financial Concerns

Each person has a unique journey and a unique financial perspective. Each one of us also behaves, feels, and thinks differently while being a member of the global human community. While each individual needs to make decisions for maximizing their opportunity for attainment of goals, there are certain factors that affect financial decisions in somewhat similar ways.

1.7.1 Lifestyle and situation

While as adults we can choose to make changes as we deem fit, many of our life's situations are often inherited or genetic or a result of circumstances where we have little or no control. Being born in Atlanta and not Sioux Falls, to a carpenter father versus a truck driver, and going to a school with a history of successful tennis players instead of musicians, are some examples.

Making your own financial decisions means you are at a stage of life where you have a modicum of control over your decisions and choices. Hence, you need to make these choices in full awareness of where you are and who you are.

1.7.2 Dependents and family situation

The structure of your family and your dependents could be an important determinant of your financial choices. It lays out the scope of your financial planning. Is the responsibility for a defined period of time or is it indefinite? Are you a sole provider or are there other providers as well? What is the prioritization of the needs of different people in the household?

The greater the responsibility towards others, the greater the tendency to seek safer havens and choices, and vice versa.

1.7.3 Nature of work and employment

Work and employment is one of the major identifying factors for most adults. They see themselves as the work they do. Career paths offer different combinations of financial benefits, security, flexibility, and growth opportunities.

Work has a complex relationship with financial planning. It is both influenced by financial planning and in turn, influences it. Some people may have been able to study for expensive college degrees as a result of financial planning done by their parents. Having graduated, the increased earning potential will now influence their own financial planning. In some cases, the choice of work could also depend on the personal situation.

1.7.4 Health

Health and well-being are increasingly important variables in our lives, a point driven home very recently by the COVID-19 pandemic. While your physical and mental composition may be a result of many factors and is subject to change very slowly, financial decisions need to be taken keeping your health situation in mind.

With rising healthcare costs, guarding against unforeseen medical needs has become a necessity for almost everyone. Prolonged illness may also require supplementing the sources of income as well as the spending habits.

1.7.5 Age bracket

All of us evolve over time. Our needs change. Our priorities change. What does not change is the goal of ensuring financial security for ourselves as well as those dependent on us.

It is important to keep in mind the requirements that may need to be provided for as one progresses in terms of age through life. Of course, one constant requirement will be to keep putting aside enough money for the time when you are not able to participate actively in the workforce and need to rely on money saved over time to maintain a standard of living that you have been used to.

Early planning years are the time to put money away to create assets that you can live off in your golden years. In the early years, though earning levels may be lower, the need to provide for dependents is also low. You can take greater risks, knowing that if they pay off it will add to your kitty, and if they do not, you still have time to recover from the shock.

Quiz

1. Which of the following are examples of financial transactions?

    a. Buying a house on cash payment

    b. Buying a house on a mortgage

    c. Renting a house

    d. All of the above

2. Which of the following does not qualify as an example of financial transactions?

    a. Buying a coffee at the streetside store on payment of cash

    b. Buying a coffee at the streetside store but on the promise of paying cash the following day

    c. Buying a coffee at the streetside store in exchange for $5 owed to you by the store from a purchase the previous day

    d. None of the above

3. Which of the following are not financial transactions?

    a. Painting on a canvas

    b. Selling the completed painting

    c. Selling the painting before it is completed

    d. All of the above

4. **The meaning of "fiat" money is** _____

   a. it is used as a store of value.

   b. its value is determined by government decree.

   c. it is used as the unit of accounting.

   d. it is the standard for deferred transactions.

5. **Social norms and widespread acceptance determine the value of a "fiat" currency.**

   a. True

   b. False

6. **Please select the most accurate statement:**

   a. Finance and money can be used interchangeably.

   b. Finance is quantified in terms of money.

   c. Money is quantified in terms of finance.

   d. Money is a wider term and includes finance.

7. **Which of the following is not a characteristic of money?**

   a. A store of value

   b. A unit of accounting

   c. The measure of the value of a currency

   d. The standard for deferred transactions

8. **Which of the following is a form in which money can be held?**

   a. Credit card

   b. Balance in bank account

   c. Checkbook

   d. None of the above

9. **Which of the following are characteristics of money? (select all the relevant ones)**

   a. A store of value

   b. A medium of exchange

   c. A unit of accounting

   d. The standard for deferred transactions

10. **Paper money is believed to have been first used in?**

    a. China

    b. Egypt

    c. US

    d. England

Answers	1 – d	2 – d	3 – a	4 – b	5 – a
	6 – b	7 – c	8 – b	9 – all correct	10 – a

Chapter Summary

◆ Personal Finance is a central thread that runs through our lives.

◆ Finance and Money are sometimes used interchangeably. Though closely related, they are different.

◆ Money has evolved over time, from holding intrinsic value such as gold coins to standardized commodity money to fiat currency, with a transition to digital currently under way.

◆ Different countries and territories have adopted different currencies with different values. This has created a foreign exchange market where currencies are bought and sold and there is a rate quoted for all pairs that can be traded.

◆ Public finance and business finance are the two other branches of finance.

◆ Each individual has a unique financial perspective based on his/ her journey and experiences. Family situation, employment and work, health and age are some of the more important variables that determine an individual's relationship with money.

This page is intentionally left blank

Chapter 2

Important Financial Concepts

Every subject has a language that is unique to it in many ways. There are words and phrases that hold a defined meaning and relevance when used in the context of the subject. An understanding of the commonly used terms and phrases becomes a prerequisite in ensuring that readers of a text reach similar understanding and conclusions. Finance is no different.

This chapter will explain some of the key concepts in finance, an understanding of which helps in understanding and managing it better.

The concepts covered are:

- Income and expense
- Income statement
- Cash flow statement

- Asset and liability

- Net worth

- Time value of money

- Compounding

2.1 Income and Expense

In the last chapter, we have seen that money is central to enabling commercial transactions to take place between individuals as well as organizations, including individual to organization transactions. As a common denominator where value can be stored, it is possible to receive money and use it for spending at a different point in time.

We are both producers as well as consumers.

2.1.1 Income

As producers, we create value through the goods and services we produce, and receive value for them in the form of money. The value we receive is defined as *income.* It could be received in the form of money, or in a form that is equivalent to money, such as the stock of the company we work for. It could also arise out of earnings from the wealth that we possess, whether created by self or received as a gift, bequest, or other means. Salary income, or wage, is one of the most common examples of income.

According to the Cornell Law School, income is "money or

value that an individual or business entity receives in exchange for providing a good or service or through investing capital."[2]

2.1.2 Expenditure

As consumers we need to fulfill our many needs, such as that of food, clothing, or housing, and acquire them by paying for them in the form of money. The value we pay for acquiring these services and goods is called *expenditure.* This could also be made in the form of money, or in a form that is equivalent to money. It could also be made from money that you don't actually possess, in the form of credit, or borrowing.

As of March 25, 2023, the Cambridge dictionary defines expenditure as "the total amount of money that an organization or person spends."

2.2 Income and Expense Statement

As responsible adults we need to ensure that we are pulling our weight in the world. One of the ways we can do this is by ensuring that our income exceeds our expenditure. In other words, we are able to generate an income that is adequate to pay for all our expenses and, hopefully, leave some money for a rainy day. Responsible execution requires a system, or process, that can be an ally in our efforts to be responsible adults.

An *income and expense statement,* also often known as the income statement, is a tool that helps us track our income and

2. "Legal Information Institute," Cornell Law School, accessed March 25, 2023, https://www.law.cornell.edu/wex/income

expenditure and keeps us on the straight and narrow. Tracking them gives us the opportunity to manage them. If we do not track, we are operating in the hope that it works out, and hope has not been known to be a reliable strategy for managing.

Look at the income and expense statement as a personal accounting statement. It records and tracks historical information, that is the items of income and expense that have already been incurred. It can be created for any period of time like a month or a quarter or a year, or even a day, depending on what your recording and tracking strategy is.

Table 2.1   Sample income and expenditure statement

Income and Expenditure Statement for	January 2023
Income	
Salary	6,000
Consulting fee	1,500
Dividend from shares	200
Total Income	7,700
Expenditure	
Food	3,000
Clothing	1,000
House rental	2,000
Total Expenditure	6,000
Net	1,700

This statement demonstrates that the person for whom it has been made has earned more than what he has spent during this period. From a personal perspective, income exceeding expenditure is a desirable objective. It enables savings that can come in handy on a rainy day.

If the income was $5,000 and not $7,000, with expenses remaining unchanged, the individual would have struggled to meet his/her expenses for the period and would have had to either resort to borrowing or dipping into savings.

Table 2.2	Sample income and expenditure statement

Income and Expenditure Statement for	January 2023
Income	
Salary	4,000
Consulting fee	1,500
Dividend from shares	200
Total Income	5,700
Expenditure	
Food	3,000
Clothing	1,000
House rental	2,000
Total Expenditure	6,000
Net	(300)

We will discuss more about income statements in the chapter on budgeting.

2.3 Cash Flow Statement

A *cash flow statement* is meant to track the inflow and outflow of cash, or money, during a defined period of time, with the net, or final figure being the amount of cash that is remaining, or available.

According to The Harvard Business School Online, the purpose of a cash flow statement is to provide a detailed picture of what happened to a business' cash during a specified period, known as the accounting period."[3]

But is that not what an income and expenditure statement also does? There is a difference. The difference is that of "recognition."

The income statement records income and expenditures based on the period they apply to. For example, if the consulting fee of $1500 shown under "income" in the income statement (Table 2.2) pertains to January 2023, it will appear in the January income statement.

However, if the arrangement with the client provides for the settlement to take place before the end of the subsequent month, the money corresponding to it will only be received in the next month.

Hence, in the cash flow statement of February, the item of $1,500 will not be included. It will only be included in the next month's cash flow statement.

Similarly, transactions that result in an inflow or outflow of cash through the assets and liabilities of the person, will also not find a way into the income statement. If you sell a house property and get $500,000 for it, it is not your income. You owned a property valued at $500,000 which you have merely converted into another asset form which is cash, or money. Hence, it will not reflect in your income statement. However, since it has generated cash from the transaction, it will find a mention in the cash

---

3. "Business Insights," Harvard Business school Online, accessed March 25, 2023, https://online.hbs.edu/blog/post/how-to-read-a-cash-flow-statement

flow statement. You now have $500,000 more cash available for whatever you may want to use it for.

In the same manner, if you borrow money, it results in an inflow of money but does not create income for you. It is something you need to pay back at some point in time. So, the amount borrowed will not find a place in the income statement but will be there in the cash flow statement. However, if there is an interest cost as a result of borrowing that amount, that will be reflected in the expenditure section of the income statement.

We will study more on this in the sections on assets and liabilities as well as net worth.

2.3.1 Components of a cash flow statement

A cash flow statement has three components. You will notice that these are in consonance with the examples of transactions shared above.

Cash flows from operating activities

These are the regular activities of the person and his/her unit or family, such as the money spent on food, clothing, entertainment, etc. Many of these transactions are likely to find a place in the income statement as well as the cash flow statement.

Cash flows from investing activities

These are activities that are in the nature of investing, either buying investments or liquidating investments made earlier that result in either an inflow or outflow of money.

Cash flows from financing activities

This comprises cash flows arising out of either borrowing money or repayment of money borrowed earlier.

2.3.2 Sample cash flow statement

Let's use the income statement of table 2.2 and add columns to include cash flow. What do we see?

| Table 2.3 | Cash flow statement superimposed on an income statement |

Income and Expenditure Statement for January 2023	Income Statement	Additional Information	Cash Flow Statement
Opening Balance			3,000
Inflow			
Salary	4,000		4,000
Consulting fee	1,500	Receivable in February	
Dividend from shares	200		200
Total Inflow	5,700		4,200
Outflows			
Food	3,000		3,000
Clothing	1,000		1,000
House rental	2,000		2,000
Loan repaid			1,000
Total Outflow	6,000		7,000
Closing Balance	(300)		200

This shows us that while we had $3,000 available with us at the beginning of the month, by the time the month ended we were down to a mere $200 available in the form of cash.

2.4 Asset and Liability

You might often find the terms assets and liabilities mentioned in the same context. Though they are the opposite of each other, together they represent the financial position of the individual or entity for whom they are being stated, with the difference of the two equating to the net worth, which we will study in the next section.

Both assets and liabilities represent a point-in-time image of the status, unlike an income statement which is for a defined period of time.

The value of an asset is as on a certain date, say January 31, and not for the month of January. The price may have remained steady for the month or it may have fluctuated. If you wish to evaluate the holding at a particular point in time, the prior movement does not count.

2.4.1 Asset

The Cornell Law School defines an asset as "something of value owned by an individual or organization."

Some common forms of assets:

- Ownership stakes in a physical property like a land parcel or a building

- Money in the bank account and certificates of deposit (CDs)

- Money owed to you by others

- Financial investments such as stocks, bonds, mutual funds, etc.

- Motor vehicles

- Personal valuables like watches, gold, diamonds, and jewelry

- Rare items such as works of art

As you can probably make out, these are items that, when it comes to the crunch, and when the owner is in dire need of money, can be liquidated to raise funds. They are stores of value in themselves. Of course, it is possible that when liquidated in a hurry, you may not be able to realize the value you believe it possesses. In some cases, the value of the holding could also be notional, such as in the case of property which is usually traded on a piece-meal basis and not through an exchange like stocks and bonds.

2.4.2 Liabilities

The English language meaning of liability is fairly wide and could vary depending on the context which can be either insurance, law, politics, or finance. For our context, which is personal finance, a liability represents an obligation to pay money or money equivalent over a future period. The total of such a future series of payment obligations can be understood as the total liability today.

The New York State Society of Certified Public Accountants[4] defines a liability as "debts or obligations owed by one entity (the debtor) to another entity (the creditor) payable in money, goods, or services."

---

4. https://www.nysscpa.org/professional-resources/accounting-terminology-guide#letterl

Some common forms of liabilities:

- Mortgage payments outstanding

- Credit card dues

- Automobile loan

- Student loan

- Taxes

2.5 Net Worth

For personal financial health, it should be clear that it is better to have a high number for your assets and a low number for your liabilities. The greater the value by which your assets exceed your liabilities, the better your financial health. This difference between assets and liabilities is known as *net worth*.

Net Worth = Assets – Liabilities

2.5.1 Balance Sheet

A *balance sheet* is a similar concept and a summary representation of assets and liabilities.

The traditional balance sheet lists down your assets and their values on one half and your liabilities along with their values on the other half. The difference between the two represents your net worth. What you also need to note here is that there is a relationship between your balance sheet and your income statement.

If you have earned a lot during a particular year and spent only a fraction of that earning, you have presumably saved money. Those savings are going to reflect in your asset picture at the end of the year, either in your bank account, in your financial investments, or in some other asset. Hence, you are likely to end up with a higher asset number at the end of the year when compared to your position at the beginning.

2.5.2 Net worth and financial position

Though an important financial construct, net worth should be considered along with other factors. Let us look at the Balance Sheet of A and B.

Table 2.4 **Personal balance sheet of A**

Assets		Liabilities	
House property	500,000	Mortgage loan	500,000
Cars	40,000	Car loan	40,000
Personal valuables	2,000	Credit card dues	10,000
Stocks and bonds	0	Student loan	100,000
Bank account	5,000		
		Net Worth	(103,000)

Table 2.5	Personal balance sheet of B		
Assets		**Liabilities**	
House property	1,000,000	Mortgage loan	0
Cars	100,000	Car loan	0
Personal valuables	500,000	Credit card dues	10,000
Stocks and bonds	2,000,000	Student loan	0
Bank account	200,000		
		Net Worth	3,790,000

Who is better placed financially? With a positive net worth of $3.79 million against a negative net worth of $103,000, clearly, B is better placed. But have you considered the possibility that A could be a recent graduate from college who has taken loans for funding the initial need for assets like a house and car while B could be a senior, retired person, living off the money collected during working years?

Table 2.6	**Annual income and expenditure statement for A**

Income and Expenditure Statement for	January 2023
Income	
Salary	200,000
Consulting fee	18,000
Dividend from shares	0
Total Income	218,000
Expenditure	
Food	30,000
Clothing	20,000
Interest on loans	40,000
Other expenses	20,000
Total Expenditure	110,000
Net	108,000

Table 2.7	**Annual income and expenditure statement for B**

Income and Expenditure Statement for	January 2023
Income	
Salary	0
Consulting fee	0
Dividend and other income from shares	100,000
Bank interest	10,000
Total Income	110,000
Expenditure	
Food	50,000
Clothing	20,000
Healthcare expenses	30,000
Other expenses	20,000
Total Expenditure	120,000
Net	(10,000)

What do we see from the above statements? We see that A, as we suspected, is starting out in life. A has a job that pays well and earns consulting income on the side. After meeting his expense requirements, he is able to contribute substantially to his net worth.

B, on the other hand, earns from the investments made over a lifetime. However, B's expenses are a little over the income, which will require him to dip into savings. As it is unlikely B will be able to increase his income, curbing expenses is something he may need to look at.

The result? Though much better off in terms of net worth, in terms of the overall financial situation, B's is not as healthy as it might have seemed. Hence, each piece of financial information contributes one perspective. In some cases, a holistic view might need to be taken.

2.6 Time Value of Money

One of the widely held beliefs about money is that it is a resource and that it comes for a price.

What does that mean? It means that a sum of money today is worth more than the same sum of money 10 years later. This is so because the sum of money if received today, can be invested to generate a return for the next 10 years. Thus, at the end of 10 years, it would become a higher amount. Hence, given a choice, I would rather get the amount today than 10 years later. The longer the available timeframe, the better the opportunity of generating a return from money.

Fun fact:

Well-known investor Warren Buffet is understood to have started his investing journey at the age of 11 when he bought 6 shares of Cities Service preferred stock—three each for his sister Doris and himself, at $38 per share, eventually selling them for $40.

When asked if he had any regrets about having started out at the age of 11, Buffet's response was that he wished he had started out earlier, presumably hinting at the time value of money and the opportunity he lost by not having done so.

2.6.1 Interest (return on money)

The time value of money is what creates the concept of interest. This is the reason interest is paid/earned on depositing money in a bank, or when a company takes a loan from a bank. The greater the rate of interest, the higher the time value of money. Of course, there are other factors that also have a bearing on the return from such a deposit or loan, such as the level of risk associated with the investment. A borrower, considered to be a riskier proposition for lenders, may need to pay a higher return to attract funds in a competitive market.

2.6.2 Compensation for foregoing use

Another way of looking at the time value of money is as compensation to the owners of the money for foregoing the use of their money for a period of time. The availability of compensation becomes a motivation for owners to let go of their money for a period of time.

2.6.3 Money as a resource

Yet another way of looking at money is as a resource. A business buys or rents the resources it requires, which could be property, manpower, and raw materials. With these resources, the business generates revenues by converting them into finished products and adding value to them. Money is another resource for this business. The business could be said to be "renting" money from a supplier for a rental fee which is called interest. When the period elapses or other conditions of the agreement are satisfied, the rented item, money, is returned to its original owner.

On the flip side, the same business could offer credit terms to its buyers, based on the time value of money for them.

2.6.4 Application to retirement

The time value of money powers most retirement plans.

If collected money would have no time value, the only option available to retirees would be to keep chipping away at the corpus built by them over their working life, and hoping that it does not run out.

The time value of money makes it possible for them to invest in different types of securities in the hope of receiving a return while keeping their corpus intact.

2.6.5 Decisions that rely on the time value of money

Many financial decisions are based on the concept of the time value of money, like

- Buying or renting a house, car, or other items

- Retirement savings

- Using savings to invest or pay down loans

The next time you hear someone say "time is money," we hope you will know exactly why.

2.7 Compounding

Albert Einstein is believed to have said that the power of compounding is the eighth wonder of the world.

What exactly is compounding? While compounding has several meanings in the English language, sticking to the context of personal finance, it can be defined as the increase in the value of an investment over time, as a result of earnings on the principal invested, as well as the earnings that periodically accrue on the principal.

In other words, not only does your principal earn interest, but the interest, once earned, also starts to earn interest. The greater the period of time over which it is permitted to flourish, the greater the beneficial impact.

2.7.1 Compound interest vs. simple interest

In simple-interest-based investments, the interest that is earned periodically is paid out to the investor for use as he/she may choose. It does not go back into the investment or account. Hence, the interest, once paid out, does not earn anything.

Compound interest, on the other hand, retains the interest

earned in the account and allows it to earn interest as well. Thus, it becomes a strategy to make your money work harder for you and grow your wealth faster.

The following table should make it clear. The comparison is for an investment of $100,000, earning at the rate of 5% per annum, with interest being paid at the end of the year.

Table 2.8	Comparison of simple and compound interest earning			
Year	Simple Interest		Compound Interest	
	Interest-earning amount	Interest	Interest-earning amount	Interest
1	100,000	5,000	100,000	5,000
2	100,000	5,000	105,000	5,250
3	100,000	5,000	110,250	5,512.5
4	100,000	5,000	115,762.5	5,788.125
5	100,000	5,000	121,550.6	6,077.531
6	100,000	5,000	127,628.2	6,381.408
7	100,000	5,000	134,009.6	6,700.478
8	100,000	5,000	140,710	7,035.502
9	100,000	5,000	147,745.5	7,387.277
10	100,000	5,000	155,132.8	7,756.641

What do we see?

- In simple interest, the amount of interest remains unchanged, as does the principal, or interest-earning amount.

- In compound interest, the interest earned in year one gets added to the principal, making the interest-earning amount for year two larger. This enables earning a larger amount of interest in year two.

- The gap keeps increasing every year.

- The simple interest being paid out is also being put to some use, even if that use is spending. So, there is value in simple interest as well. It may well be the objective of the investor to get a certain amount back every year to meet expenses. However, by being paid out, it becomes ineligible for earning, creating the benefit of compound interest.

Let us take another case to understand the beneficial impact of compounding over longer durations. In both cases in this example, a total of $200,000 is deposited over a 20-year timeframe.

Situation one – $10,000 is deposited every year.

Situation two – $20,000 is deposited every year from the 11th year to the 20th year.

| Table 2.9 | Benefit of compounding over longer tenures |

	Situation 1			Situation 2		
Year	Amount deposited	Total interest-earning Amount	Interest	Amount deposited	Total interest-earning amount	Interest
1	10,000	10,000	500	0	0	0
2	10,000	20,500	1,025	0	0	0
3	10,000	31,525	1,576.25	0	0	0
4	10,000	43,101.25	2,155.063	0	0	0
5	10,000	55,256.31	2,762.816	0	0	0
6	10,000	68,019.13	3,400.956	0	0	0
7	10,000	81,420.08	4,071.004	0	0	0
8	10,000	95,491.09	4,774.554	0	0	0
9	10,000	110,265.6	5,513.282	0	0	0
10	10,000	125,778.9	6,288.946	0	0	0
11	10,000	142,067.9	7,103.394	20,000	20,000	1,000
12	10,000	159,171.3	7,958.563	20,000	41,000	2,050
13	10,000	177,129.8	8,856.491	20,000	63,050	3,152.5
14	10,000	195,986.3	9,799.316	20,000	86,202.5	4,310.125
15	10,000	215,785.6	10,789.28	20,000	110,512.6	5,525.631
16	10,000	236,574.9	11,828.75	20,000	136,038.3	6,801.913
17	10,000	258,403.7	12,920.18	20,000	162,840.2	8,142.008
18	10,000	281,323.8	14,066.19	20,000	190,982.2	9,549.109
19	10,000	305,390	15,269.5	20,000	220,531.3	11,026.56
20	10,000	330,659.5	16,532.98	20,000	251,557.9	12,577.89
Total	200,000		14,7192.5	200,000		64,135.74

What do we see? Situation one earns a total interest of $147,192.50 while situation 2 earns $64,135.74, less than half, even though the total amount invested is the same in both cases.

Let us create situation three, in which the 20,000 per year is invested for the first 10 years, and nothing for years 11 to 20. What is the result?

Table 2.10 **Benefit of compounding by investing earlier**

Situation 3

Year	Amount deposited	Total interest-earning Amount	Interest
1	20,000	20,000	1,000
2	20,000	41,000	2,050
3	20,000	63,050	3,152.5
4	20,000	86,202.5	4,310.125
5	20,000	110,512.6	5,525.631
6	20,000	136,038.3	6,801.913
7	20,000	162,840.2	8,142.008
8	20,000	190,982.2	9,549.109
9	20,000	220,531.3	11,026.56
10	20,000	251,557.9	12,577.89
11		264,135.7	13,206.79
12		277,342.5	13,867.13
13		291,209.7	14,560.48
14		305,770.1	15,288.51
15		321,058.6	16,052.93
16		337,111.6	16,855.58
17		353,967.2	17,698.36
18		371,665.5	18,583.28
19		390,248.8	19,512.44
20		409,761.2	20,488.06
Total	200,000		230,249.3

The total interest earned at the end of the 20th year stands at $230,249.30, the highest among the 3 scenarios.

The learning:

- Invest early

- Invest more and invest early

Quiz

1. Income is what we receive as value for the goods and services we produce.

   a. True

   b. False

2. It is normal human behavior to desire that one's expenditure should exceed one's income at all points in time.

   a. Agree

   b. Disagree

3. Which of the following methods of purchasing qualify as expenditure?

   a. Credit card

   b. Cash

   c. Check

   d. All of the above

4. **An income and expense statement tracks transactions that**

    _____

    a. have happened in the past month.

    b. have happened in the past 12 months.

    c. have happened in any specified past period of time.

    d. will happen in the future.

5. **Compounding will have a greater impact over a shorter period of time:**

    a. True

    b. False

6. **An expenditure could be incurred today out of money that you don't actually possess.**

    a. True

    b. False

7. **An income and expenditure statement tracks which of the following items? (You can choose more than one)**

    a. Assets

    b. Liabilities

    c. Income

    d. Expenditure

8. **A personal balance sheet reflects which of the following items? (You can choose more than one)**

   a. Assets

   b. Liabilities

   c. Income

   d. Expenditure

9. **A personal balance sheet reflects** _____

   a. point in time position of income and expenditure.

   b. transactions over a defined period in assets and liabilities.

   c. point in time position of assets and liabilities.

   d. transactions over a defined period in income and expenditure.

10. **A cash flow statement is** _____

   a. an income and expenditure statement by another name.

   b. a balance sheet by another name.

   c. a position of net worth by another name.

   d. None of the above

Answers	1 – a	2 – b	3 – d	4 – c	5 – b
	6 – a	7 – c, d	8 – a, b	9 – c	10 – d

Chapter Summary

◆ An understanding of key terms is essential to the understanding of personal finance.

◆ We create goods and services and receive value for them in the form of money. The value we receive is defined as income. The value we pay for acquiring services and goods is called expenditure.

◆ An income and expense statement helps us track our income and expenditure and stay within budget.

◆ A cash flow statement is similar but tracks actual inflows and outflows of cash.

◆ Assets represent something of value owned by an individual or business.

◆ Liabilities represent what the individual owes to another.

◆ Net worth represents the difference between assets and liabilities. Assets higher than liabilities mean positive net worth, and vice versa.

◆ The value of money today is greater than its value later. In other words, the same amount of money can purchase a greater set of goods than it can several years later.

◆ Compounding of interest means earning interest on interest already earned. Compounding leads to a more rapid appreciation of an investment than simple interest.

Chapter 3

Budgeting

This chapter introduces the concept of financial planning which is carried out in the form of the budgeting process. Budgeting is a process through which a realistic, desired financial path is constructed with the objective of yielding the best possible financial outcomes. The real-life outcomes are compared against the budgeted pathway at periodic intervals with a view of analyzing the variances as well as course correcting. It is also possible that there is a change in the underlying fundamental assumptions which could result in the budget (for the remaining period) being updated.

Other concepts related to the budgeting process are also covered, such as:

- The importance of planning
- Introduction to a budget
- Principles of good budgeting
- Common budgeting methods

- Creating a budget
- Contingency Planning

3.1 The Importance of Planning

One of the truisms of life is that the decisions one makes today can only impact the future. There is no way we can influence what has happened in the past. This truism requires us to make responsible decisions, in order that they result in outcomes that take us closer to the goals we have defined and to achieve what we have been striving for.

One individual may want to travel overseas every year. Another may want to live in a palace while yet another may want to retire at 40. Goals vary with individuals and each individual can have many different goals. This is where financial planning comes into the picture.

Our finances are a common thread that runs through most aspects of our life. Earning, spending, investing, borrowing, and lending are all financial decisions. Hence, we need to be judicious in making decisions regarding finance. We need to ensure that our decisions are able to place us in the best position possible to achieve what we want to achieve.

Of course, it is also possible that the planning process helps us realize that not all of our goals can be met. This knowledge not only prepares us in advance for disappointment but also helps us in making choices between different goals. Hence, in short, the planning process aids our decision-making process and equips us to make better-quality decisions.

3.2 Introduction to a Budget

A financial plan is also known as a *budget.* It is a prospective view of how your financial situation is expected to play out over the planning period, whether it is monthly, quarterly, yearly, or any other. It enables you to plan. Looked at another way, it could be understood as an income and expenditure statement created in advance.

We came across this sample statement in Chapter 2:

Table 3.1	Sample income and expenditure statement

Income and Expenditure Statement for	January 2023
Income	
Salary	6,000
Consulting fee	1,500
Dividend from shares	200
Total Income	7,700
Expenditure	
Food	3,000
Clothing	1,000
House rental	2,000
Total Expenditure	6,000
Net	1,700

This statement was compiled at the end of the month when the actual amounts and categories were known. If we were at the end of December and trying to visualize and document what our January income and expense statement would look like when we finally compiled all the data at the end of January, we would be creating a budget.

If we had created a budget for January that would exactly match the actuals at the end of January, it would give us great confidence in our planning and budgeting process.

3.2.1 Types of budgets

We have earlier seen that we can create:

- An income statement that tells you about your income and expenditure during a certain period of time

- A cash flow statement that informs us about the availability of cash (or funds) and how it has moved during a period

We can also create a budget that mirrors one of the two or both. It depends on how you wish to manage your finances.

3.3 Principles of Good Budgeting

3.3.1 A budget is a living document and should be updated as and when there is a need

For example, if you are forced to spend a large amount on an unplanned item, say related to a family member's health, that had not been budgeted, it means you will have less money available in the future. If you don't update the budget to reflect this fact and try to economize on future expenses, you could end up spending more than you have.

3.3.2 Pause, think, and evaluate the assumptions periodically

As a corollary to the above, there is a need to evaluate and assess the underlying assumptions based on which the budget has been built. The pausing and rethinking should also take into account any new uncertainties that now seem to loom on the horizon which did not exist the last time such an exercise was done.

3.3.3 A budget should be the most realistic estimate of future finances

A budget is not created based on what you would like in the future, such as a trip to the moon or an income like Jeff Bezos, but what you believe is the most likely situation. There is no scope for hope or wishful thinking while budgeting. You need to be as objective and truthful with yourself as you can be. It is better to get the bad news today when you still have an opportunity to move things around, than at the end of the period.

3.3.4 Faithful tracking of income and expenses leads to better budgeting

A budget is not something that is made and then forgotten. It is a tool for your decision-making. The budget is made more robust when you track the actual events against the plan. Even if you have gone wrong in budgeting during this cycle, tracking financial flows against the budget will help you become better and better in the course of time.

3.3.5 When in doubt, be conservative

As in accounting, so in budgeting. A budget is supposed to be a realistic projection of your financial situation for a future period of time. While, with experience, you will get better at it and reduce the gap between the budget and actual performance, you could be uncertain about events while budgeting.

Will I earn $1,000 as consulting income or will it be $2,000? Will my flight ticket cost $300 or will it cost $500? A safe approach, or conservatism, is recommended for such items where you are uncertain. It will result in pleasant surprises instead of nasty ones as the real situation unfolds.

3.4 Common Budgeting Methods

Budgets can be created in different ways, based on your personal situation as well as your level of comfort. Remember, it is something you need to do repeatedly, hence doing it in a manner that makes you comfortable will perhaps be your best chance of doing it repeatedly. The five most common methods are described below:

3.4.1 Zero-base budget

In this format, you account for every penny that is coming in with the pennies going out. If your income exceeds your expenses, the leftover amount is allocated to savings. If your expense exceeds your income, the shortfall is made up through borrowings. Thus, there is no "remainder" on either side of the budget sheet.

This method works well for people interested in tracking their finances closely, down to pennies, and ensuring each one is accounted for. It also works well for people with a high degree of predictability in income as well as expenses.

3.4.2 50/30/20 budget

50/30/20[5] is a prescriptive format that specifies benchmarks for how much you should spend on different items, namely needs, wants, and savings. As can perhaps be guessed by the name, this method suggests that the following should be the breakup of income allocation:

50% – on needs which would be the most basic requirements such as shelter, food, clothing, etc.

30% – on wants; in other words, items not essential to be purchased but ones that you desire, such as show tickets, entertainment, travel, etc.

20% – on creating savings for meeting future needs as well as emergency funds.

---

5. Elizabeth Warren, Amelia W. Tyagi. 2006. "All Your Worth: The Ultimate Lifetime Money Plan." (Free Press)

This format has been recommended for first-timers who are looking for a framework to start managing their finances. It may not be suitable for people who need to allocate a substantial portion of their income towards debt repayment.

3.4.3 Pay yourself first

This is a variation of the 50/30/20 method. In fact, this is sometimes referred to as the 80/20 budget with 20 being savings and 80 everything else.

In this method, priority is given to savings for the future on the understanding that current needs could consume the entire income, leaving nothing for a rainy day. Hence, the greatest importance in allocating money has to be towards savings.

You can choose between allocating a lump sum towards this 'future' envelope or a percentage of income. Once that has been done, you will find greater mental freedom in spending on the current items of need.

3.4.4 The envelope method

As the name suggests, in this method, money is allocated towards different expenses right upfront during the planning period. An "envelope" might suggest keeping cash in distinct envelopes marked with the name of the cost head, and that is the intention. Spending while you still have cash in your hands is generally considered to be a safe way to avoid overspending, which modern tools like credit cards often lead us to.

With payment systems going cashless, the modern individual or householder may prefer a variation in the form of accounting "envelopes" into which the money goes, even though there is a greater risk of overspending. This could be suitable for people trying to pay off debt and have a chunky envelope for it.

3.4.5 Priority-based budget

This is sometimes also referred to as the "mindful" budget where decisions are taken consciously, as opposed to some other methods of budgeting that have been suggested to overcome human frailties.

This is, in some ways, how organizations might create a budget to match organizational goals. This is for the mature individual who is able to recognize and understand human limitations and work with them to achieve the best results. There are no taboos and there are no certainties. The budget-maker decides where the money is best spent, creates a budget accordingly, and hopefully, spends in line with the budget created.

3.5 Creating a Budget

How does one create a budget?

The process requires the budget-maker to be able to project his/her life forward through the budget period and quantify the impact of choices and decisions in financial terms.

We will divide this discussion into two parts:

1. Repeat budgets – for people who have created a budget in the past and do not have a substantial change in their lifestyle

2. First-time budgets – for people either creating the first budget or whose lifestyle has undergone a significant change since the last budget

3.5.1 Repeat budgets

If you have made a budget for an earlier period and your life is expected to continue along mostly similar lines, it should be a relatively straightforward process for you.

Let us go back to the income and expense statement referenced earlier.

Table 3.2	Sample income and expenditure statement

Income and Expenditure Statement for	January 2023
Income	
Salary	6,000
Consulting fee	1,500
Dividend from shares	200
Total Income	7,700
Expenditure	
Food	3,000
Clothing	1,000
House rental	2,000
Total Expenditure	6,000
Net	1,700

We already have the actual information for January.

If we now set out to create a budget for February, we can use this information as a baseline, and make changes based upon our expectation of what might happen. If we don't foresee any changes, we could even retain the same numbers.

| Table 3.3 | Budget for February 2023 |

Income and Expenditure Statement for	January 2023	Budget for February 2023	Reason
Income			
Salary	6,000	6,000	
Consulting fee	1,500	1,500	
Dividend from shares	200	200	
Total Income	7,700	7,700	
Expenditure			
Food	3,000	4,000	House guests expected
Clothing	1,000	1,000	
House rental	2,000	2,000	
Total Expenditure	6,000	7,000	
Net	1,700	700	

A question — assume you had access to the budget that had been made in December for January, along with the actual numbers for January:

| Table 3.4 | Sample income and expenditure statement |

Income and Expenditure Statement for	Budget for January 2023	January 2023 actuals
Income		
Salary	6,000	6,000
Consulting fee	2,500	1,500
Dividend from shares	200	200
Total Income	8,700	7,700
Expenditure		
Food	3,000	3,000
Clothing	1,000	1,000
House rental	2,000	2,000
Total Expenditure	6,000	6,000
Net	2,700	1,700

The difference between the budget and actuals for January 2023 is that the actual consulting fee earned is 1,500 instead of the budgeted 2,500. This reduced the Net from a budgeted figure of 2,700 to 1,700.

What would you use for your February budget exercise? The January budget that was created in December or the January actuals? The answer is – January actuals.

The budget was an estimate or projection. What really happened is captured in the actual numbers. And that forms the most substantive basis for any future budget. Any additional information you have should be built on top of the actual numbers.

3.5.2 First-time budgets

What about first-time budgets?

If you have conducted financial transactions earlier and maintained an income and expense statement, it could provide a starting point even if you have not created a budget earlier. However, what if you have not created a budget earlier or maintained an income and expense statement?

There does not seem any alternative to the method of "ground-up" thinking. It will require thinking and reflecting upon the future period of time for which you plan to make a budget and how it is likely to turn out. Of course, it may also require reflection upon the past in the hope of learning from it for the future.

Once created, it will become the pillar against which actual performance can be tracked and future budgets created.

3.6 Contingency Planning

"The best-laid plans of mice and men often go awry."[6]

Contingency planning is the process of trying to ensure that when unforeseen situations and events occur, it does not push your carefully planned life off the rails. Is it possible to plan for contingencies? After all, is the budgeting exercise in itself not an effort at converting the future unknowns to knowns?

Some people argue that contingencies are, by their very nature, extreme events that can neither be predicted nor planned for.

---

6. Burns, Robert, To A Mouse (1785)

Could anyone have built the ramifications of COVID-19 in their financial planning if they were creating a plan for 2020 in the last quarter of 2019? Perhaps not.

Predicting future events, perhaps, is not even the objective of contingency planning. Contingency planning only seeks to ensure that at the individual or family unit level, the level at which financial planning is being done, there is adequate flexibility in the financial management system that is able to withstand the fallout of such extreme events.

Moreover, as a planner, it is also up to you to decide how deep you wish to go into the assumptions as well as look out into the future, to underpin your planning. The greater the awareness and mindfulness with which the exercise is carried out, the better the prospects of it becoming a useful tool.

But, how exactly does one build future unknown events into the planning process? By applying the principles of good budgeting that have been shared earlier and are summarized below:

- A budget is a living document and should be updated as and when there is a need.

- Pause, think, and evaluate the assumptions periodically.

- A budget should be the most realistic estimate of future finances.

- Faithful tracking of income and expenses leads to better budgeting.

- When in doubt, be conservative.

The best way to handle a contingency is by ensuring that it does not materialize. Unforeseen events may happen, but a robust financial planning process will prevent it from becoming a contingency. At the very least, the creation of a "contingency fund" is recommended, which could help you tide over a period during which income is uncertain or absent.

So what should be the size of the contingency fund?

There cannot be a single answer. It will obviously depend on your situation in life as well as your lifestyle. In fact, at retirement, the corpus built up is a contingency fund for the rest of the retired life. At an earlier stage of life, it will depend on how long are the "no income" periods. If you're still uncertain about the size of the fund, try to work with a contingency fund equal to three months of expenses, to begin with. As you gain experience about its adequacy, you can make changes.

Quiz

1. **The decisions we take today impact the _____.**

   a. past

   b. present

   c. future

   d. All of the above

2. **One individual can have _____**

   a. only one financial goal.

   b. up to five financial goals.

   c. multiple (any number of) financial goals.

3. **Financial planning can be done when an individual has**

   _____

   a. only one financial goal.

   b. up to five financial goals.

   c. any number of financial goals.

   d. individuals do not do financial planning.

4. **Budgeting is an exercise for organizations and not for individuals.**

    a. True

    b. False

5. **The process of budgeting can help us understand which of our goals are achievable and which are not.**

    a. True

    b. False

6. **Which of the following would we not find in a budget for next year?**

    a. Expected income from salary

    b. An uncle dies and bequeaths money

    c. Food expenses

    d. Medical insurance premium

7. **A budget is prepared for a _____**

    a. past period of time.

    b. present period of time.

    c. future period of time.

    d. None of the above.

8. **A budgeting exercise could be considered to be most successful if** _____

   a. the actuals are lower than the budget.

   b. the actuals are higher than the budget.

   c. the actuals closely match the budget.

   d. All of the above

9. **A budget should be** _____

   a. the most optimistic account of future events.

   b. the most pessimistic account of future events.

   c. the most realistic account of future events.

10. **Which of the following could be considered the most suitable starting point for a repeat budget?**

   a. The balance sheet for the most recent period

   b. The budget for the previous period

   c. The income and expense statement for the period immediately preceding the last period

   d. The income and expense statement for the most recent period

Answers	1 – c	2 – c	3 – c	4 – b	5 – a
	6 – b	7 – c	8 – c	9 – c	10 – d

Chapter Summary

◆ In this chapter, we covered some fundamental concepts which are essential to the understanding of the financial planning process.

◆ The planning process aids our decision-making process and equips us to make better-quality decisions.

◆ A budget is a financial plan of how we see a future period in financial terms.

◆ A budget should be realistic. It should be evaluated periodically and updated as and when the need is felt.

◆ There are several methods for budgeting.

◆ Creating a budget the first time can be a challenging exercise.

◆ Budgets should have an element of contingency built in.

This page is intentionally left blank

Chapter 4

Banking

This chapter introduces the concept of banking and its role in managing money and utilizing it effectively. Banks are institutions where the stock in trade is money. They hold our money, keep it safe, enable us to earn interest on the money, and also transfer it from one place and account to another. Digitalization is bringing in a fresh set of players such as digital banks into the equation, forcing traditional banks to rethink strategies.

The key learning objectives of this chapter include understanding the following:

- Types of banks, including central banks and their role

- Types of accounts that banks offer

- Credit facilities offered by banks and the different ways of classifying them based on the type of facility, secured or unsecured, purpose, and type of rate of interest

- Other facilities offered by banks such as payments, cash services and safe deposit boxes

4.1 Introduction to Banking

We have seen in earlier chapters how money is an integral part of the modern world. As a key resource, money also needs to be handled with care and efficiency, so that the beneficial outcomes resulting from it can be maximized.

This is where a bank comes into the picture. It can be described as an organization that deals in money. People (and non-people entities) who have excess money can deposit it with a bank and earn interest on it.

But how does a bank pay interest? By earning through the expedient of deploying it effectively.

People who have a need for money for their requirements can approach a bank for it. The bank will evaluate the need and their ability to repay the money. If satisfied, the bank will give them the money in the form of an advance or a loan. In return for the facility, the bank will charge interest on the money so advanced.

Without a bank to facilitate:

- The person who has excess money will neither know what to do with it nor be able to earn from it.

- The person who needs money will not know who to approach for the money needed.

- If these two do finally discover each other, the lender will not know how to evaluate the project and whether the borrower will be in a position to return the money.

A bank steps into this vacuum and becomes the facilitator for all things money.

With a bank in the picture:

- A person with excess money can go to the bank and deposit it there, and earn interest on it.

- A person with the need for money can approach the bank for funds.

- The bank will evaluate the proposal and decide whether to extend credit to him or not, and on what terms.

Since banking is run as a private enterprise, there could be many banks operating in a jurisdiction. Individually they will not have access to the complete market in terms of depositors and borrowers, but enough to satisfy the banking needs of most people and organizations.

4.2 Types of Banks

There are various types of banks that you might come across. The most common ones are:

4.2.1 Commercial banks

These are the banks that we will encounter in marketplaces and streetside locations. Commercial banks are the ones carrying out the day-to-day transactions like deposit-taking and loan-making that we understand as the primary function of banks. They can also be called fund-based banks that seek deposits from customers and make loans to other customers and earn based on the difference between the two rates, apart from charging fees on some services. These banks are usually further classified based on the type of customers they deal with and could offer products and services more suited to the requirements of the customer set they cater to. The two types of commercial banks are:

1. **Retail banks**
   These banks are also known as consumer banks and deal mostly with the banking requirements of individuals.

2. **Corporate Banks**
   These banks are also known as corporate and institutional banks and deal with the banking requirements of businesses, from small to large.

4.2.2 Investment banks

The remit of investment banks is providing complex financial services, mainly to large corporations and acting as financial intermediaries. Unlike commercial banks, their revenue comes from fee-based and trading-related activities.

Some examples of the services they offer are:

- Underwriting and management of IPOs
- Assistance with mergers and acquisitions
- Trading of stocks, bonds, and other securities between companies and investors
- Managing investment portfolios

- Raising money for specific purposes on behalf of businesses as well as governments

- Facilitating the raising of capital through debt and equity

Fun facts: From the federal reserve archives[7]

In the wake of the 1929 stock market crash and the subsequent Great Depression, Congress was concerned that commercial banking operations and the payments system were incurring losses from volatile equity markets. An important motivation for the act was the desire to restrict the use of bank credit for speculation and to direct bank credit into what Glass and others thought to be more productive uses, such as industry, commerce, and agriculture.

In response to these concerns, the main provisions of the Banking Act of 1933 effectively separated commercial banking from investment banking. Senator Glass was the driving force behind this provision. Basically, commercial banks, which took in deposits and made loans, were no longer allowed to underwrite or deal in securities, while investment banks, which underwrote and dealt in securities, were no longer allowed to have close connections to commercial banks, such as overlapping directorships or common ownership.

In 1999, however, the act was repealed and replaced with the Gramm-Leach-Bliley Act, allowing commercial banks to offer investment banking services again.

---

7. "Banking Act of 1933 (Glass-Steagall)," Federal Rederve History, June 16, 1933, https://www.federalreservehistory.org/essays/glass-steagall-act#:~:text=The%20 Glass%2DSteagall%20Act%20effectively,law%20by%20President%20Franklin%20D

4.2.3 Savings and loan associations

Though technically not banks, savings and loan associations, or S&Ls, offer fairly similar products which include taking deposits and making loans, mainly mortgages.

They are also known as thrifts or savings associations and are owned and overseen by their members, like a cooperative. Hence, they have been able to pay out better rates of interest on deposits placed by their customers, creating an attraction for members to bank with them.

4.2.4 Credit unions

A credit union is a nonprofit organization owned by people who use its financial products. The money paid by members to purchase shares of the union is the corpus for making loans to its members on which interest is charged. It is a self-managed organization with a board elected by members. Without the need to distribute profits to shareholders, credit unions can offer better terms on products that are common with banks, such as credit cards and personal loans. Credit unions often define criteria for membership, which is not open to all.

4.2.5 Online banks

The digital revolution of the 21st century has had an expected impact on banking; many of its services have gone digital. Digital delivery of banking services has been a blessing for commercial banks, who have been able to economize on the need for expensive real estate and manpower to handle customer requirements. Most normal banking transactions such as account opening, account closing, transferring money, etc. can be done online. It is known as online banking or net banking.

Taking the revolution to the next level are online banks, which do not shy away from having no physical presence whatsoever. They are known as online-only, internet-only, or direct banks. They are becoming increasingly popular because they are able to offer better fees and interest rates as a result of being a lower-cost operation.

4.2.6 Central Banks

Central Banks are the ones who keep the complex network of financial institutions, and the financial system, humming. They do not interact directly with the public but make policies and regulations for banks that do.

They are responsible for the economic system in its entirety, including the stability of the currency and the health of financial organizations.

The US central bank is the Federal Reserve Bank. One of its policies that catches the attention of the public is that of rate adjustment to control the money supply.

4.3 Types of Accounts

Banks offer several types of accounts to meet the safekeeping, earning, and transactional needs of customers. The most common ones are:

4.3.1 Checking account

This is an account into which you deposit your money. Once deposited, your money shows up as a balance in your account statement. You can generally draw all the money you have in the account, subject to specific conditions the bank may impose.

The checking account got its name from the "checking" facility which was an important feature of banking before digital banking became the norm. A "check" is a paper instrument that could be used by the account holder to pay someone simply by writing the amount and the beneficiary's name on it. The beneficiary would then realize the funds through his bank in a settlement process between banks known as "clearing."

The traditional checking account did not earn interest on balances and could have a maintenance fee levied on it as well as minimum balance maintenance stipulations. However, in order to attract customers, banks have been experimenting with payment of interest in different forms on checking account balances.

4.3.2 Savings account

A savings account could be considered as a variant of the checking account. In fact, the two together can be called "transactional" accounts, in which deposit and withdrawal transactions can be conducted.

Savings accounts were designed to encourage the habit of saving among people. Hence, the way they are set up encourages deposit transactions more than withdrawal ones. For instance, savings accounts earn interest on their balances. The traditional savings account does not come with a checkbook. This limits the methods through which money could be withdrawn from the account. Besides, the number of withdrawals in a month is limited.

Customers track the money they have saved through their account statements. They may also have minimum balance maintenance stipulations as well as periodic account management fees.

Banks offering savings accounts have been experimenting with solutions to offer additional facilities on savings accounts in order to attract customers.

4.3.3 Certificate of deposit

A certificate of deposit (CD) is a time deposit account. In this type of account, you confirm to the bank that the amount placed in a CD will continue to be with the bank, and not withdrawn, till the maturity date on the certificate.

This assurance enables the bank to deploy the amount more effectively. The higher return they are able to earn gets shared with the customer in the form of interest that is higher than a savings account. Withdrawal of money from a CD is not entirely prohibited but is usually subject to certain premature withdrawal penalties. Many bank customers who use CDs prefer to use a strategy known as a CD ladder. They build a portfolio of multiple CDs with different maturity dates that coincide with the dates on which they expect to have a need for those funds.

With a CD, you can earn interest that is better than a savings account, but with reduced control over withdrawal. It is suitable for money that you are reasonably certain you will not need for a period of time. Also, the interest is not dependent on the value of an underlying security, like stocks. The CD amount and return are definite, as agreed at the time of opening the account.

4.3.4 Money market account

A money market account (MMA) seeks to combine the features of a checking account and a savings account for customers and has established itself as a unique product offering.

Customers get check writing and debit card withdrawal facilities while earning interest on an MMA account. The entry criteria and requirements for account opening, usually in the form of a minimum balance for account opening as well as for regular maintenance, are likely to be higher for an MMA account.

The applicable rate of interest could vary with the amount in the account, with higher balances earning higher rates.

Fun facts: Bank accounts are insured by the Federal Deposit Insurance Corporation[8]

FDIC deposit insurance protects bank customers in the event that an FDIC-insured depository institution fails. Bank customers don't need to purchase deposit insurance; it is automatic for any deposit account opened at an FDIC-insured bank. Deposits are insured up to at least $250,000 per depositor, per FDIC-insured bank, per ownership category.

FDIC deposit insurance only covers certain deposit products, such as checking and savings accounts, money market deposit accounts (MMDAs), and certificates of deposit (CDs).

---

8. "Deposit Insurance FAQs," Resources, FDIC, last updated March 20, 2023, https://www.fdic.gov/resources/deposit-insurance/faq/index.html

4.4 Lending Facilities

Lending, or making loans, could be considered as the business side of banks. Lending is what generates income for them, with which they are able to pay interest to depositors and meet their own expenses. Lending is also referred to as credit or advances.

There are many ways in which banks make loans. There are also many ways of classifying lending. The most common ones are:

4.4.1 Based on the type of facility:

Account overdraft

A bank will typically honor payment requests in an account to the extent of availability of funds in it. At times, the bank will agree to a request from an account holder to honor payment requests beyond the available amount.

This is known as an overdraft arrangement and is generally applicable to business or related activities. It protects the business against a temporary shortfall in funds. It is an arrangement the bank might agree to if satisfied that the money it is paying on behalf of the client will be returned. Such overdrafts are eligible for being charged interest.

Loan

A loan is a fixed amount granted up front which then keeps getting paid off over an agreed term in the form of equated monthly installments (EMIs) that include interest. Some of the most popular types of consumer lending are done in the form of loans, with mortgage loans and auto loans being widely used.

Revolving credit

A credit card is the most common form of this type of lending. In some ways, it is similar to the overdraft facility in that it lets the borrower decide when to draw how much. Where it differs is that periodically, typically monthly, credit card dues have to be either paid off or they begin to attract steep rates of interest till cleared. Today, almost everyone who has a credit score that makes him eligible has a credit card.

4.4.2 Based on security

Secured loan

If the lending arrangement is based on the security of an asset that could be sold to recover the outstanding amount in the event of borrower default, it is known as a secured facility. A mortgage loan is a well-known type of secured facility. In the event of borrower default, the lender can force its sale for recovering dues.

Unsecured loan

When the lender does not have access to an asset that could be sold to recover unpaid dues, the arrangement is known as an unsecured facility. Credit cards are generally issued without an asset backing up the facility. Unsecured loans typically are more expensive compared to secured loans as the bank carries a higher risk of financial loss.

4.4.3 Based on purpose

Many loans have a specific purpose and are best defined in terms of that purpose. Some such loans are:

- Housing loans
- Auto loans
- Student loans
- Medical loans
- Payday loans
- Wedding loans

4.4.4 Based on the type of interest

Fixed rate loan

The rate of interest does not change during the tenure of the loan.

Variable rate loan

The interest is pegged to an external benchmark such as the "prime rate" and changes when the benchmark rate changes.

4.5 Other Banking Services

4.5.1 Cash and ATM services

With the advent of online banking and transaction capability, the relevance of cash availability has been reduced. Nevertheless, most people feel comfortable with some dollars in their wallets for meeting emergency requirements.

Traditional banks make cash deposit and withdrawal services available through their branches. Cash withdrawal is mostly limited to automated teller machines (ATMs) that can be accessed through a debit card. Cash withdrawal can also be done at non-bank locations that have an ATM.

4.5.2 Payments

Moving money around is another major function of banks.

Checks

Checks have been a popular mechanism for effecting money transfers. All you needed to do was issue a check favoring the person or organization you needed to make the payment to. The beneficiary would deposit the check in his bank and his bank would realize the funds through the interbank clearing system in place. But with the rise of online banking, check usage is gradually reducing.

Online banking

Access to online banking enables account holders to transfer money into the account of almost any bank account holder in the jurisdiction if they have the correct payee details available.

Wire transfers

Before online banking, wire transfers were the accepted method of transferring money through an interbank money transfer system. With the advent of online banking, the need for wire transfers through a bank has been reduced. The need for international wire transfers, however, continues.

> **Fun fact:**
>
> Cross-border wire transfers rely on the backbone of the SWIFT messaging system. SWIFT stands for the Society for Worldwide Interbank Financial Telecommunication. [9]
>
> Swift's messaging services are trusted and used by more than 11,000 financial institutions in more than 200 countries and territories around the world. Providing reliable, secure, and efficient messaging services to the community of users, Swift is the backbone of global financial communication.

4.5.3 Safe deposit boxes

A safe deposit box is a secure container that branches of some banks offer to customers. They can be rented for safekeeping of valuables. They are typically secured by multiple locking

---

9. "Messaging and Standards," Discover SWIFT, SWIFT, accessed on August 2, 2023, https://www.swift.com/about-us/discover-swift/messaging-and-standards

arrangements and kept inside the highly secure bank vault at the locations they are offered.

It must be noted, however, that FDIC insurance protection does not cover safe deposit boxes.

4.5.4 Investing and wealth management

As financial supermarkets, banks are well placed to offer investment and wealth management-related services to their customers.

Wealth management services aim to help individuals acquire, protect, and grow their wealth. It covers advisory services on investment choices as well as tax, retirement, and estate-related planning. Banks could also offer investment-related products for purchase by their clients.

Quiz

1. **Which of the following problems would arise if there were no banks?**

   a. The person who has excess money will neither know what to do with it nor be able to earn from it.

   b. The person who needs money will not know who to approach for the money needed.

   c. If these two do finally discover each other, the lender will not know how to evaluate the project and whether the borrower will be in a position to return the money.

   d. All three of the above

   e. None of the above three

2. **Every bank operating in a place has access to the complete market in terms of depositors and borrowers.**

   a. True

   b. False

3. **A retail bank is a specific kind of which type of bank?**

   a. Commercial bank

   b. Investment bank

   c. Credit union

   d. Central bank

4. **Which of the following financial institutions deal mostly with the financial needs of individuals? (Select all applicable)**

   a. Retail banks

   b. Investment banks

   c. Credit unions

   d. Central banks

5. **Which of the following types of banks mostly deal with the banking requirements of businesses, corporations, and institutions?**

   a. Retail banks

   b. Investment banks

   c. Credit unions

   d. Central banks

6. **For which type of bank is the primary income source the difference between interest earned from borrowers and interest paid to depositors?**

   a. Commercial banks

   b. Investment banks

   c. Credit unions

   d. None of the above

7. **Which of the following are among the major activities of investment banks? (Select all applicable)**

   a. Underwriting and management of IPOs

   b. Making mortgage loans

   c. Assistance with mergers and acquisitions

   d. Online funds transfer

8. **A separation of commercial banking and investment banking was engineered by which act?**

   a. Glass-Steagall Act

   b. Gramm-Leach-Bliley Act

   c. Central Banking Act

   d. Frank-Dodd Act

9. **In the present banking environment, commercial banking and investment banking services can be offered under the same bank.**

   a. True

   b. False

10. Which of the following institutions operate as cooperatives? (Select all applicable)

   a. Commercial banks

   b. Credit unions

   c. Savings and loan associations

   d. Online banks

Answers	1 – d	2 – b	3 – a	4 – a, c	5 – b
	6 – a	7 – a, c	8 – a	9 – a	10 – b, c

Chapter Summary

In this chapter, we introduced the concept of banking and discussed various aspects of banking.

◆ Banks can be of different types, such as commercial banks, investment banks, savings and loan institutions, credit unions, online banks, and central banks.

◆ Customers can hold many different types of accounts in a bank, each for a specific use and objective, such as checking accounts, savings accounts, certificates of deposit, and money market accounts.

◆ Banks also offer credit to their customers, subject to their evaluation criteria being satisfied.

◆ In addition to keeping customers' money and lending money to them, banks offer many other services such as payments, cash services, and safe deposit boxes.

This page is intentionally left blank

Chapter 5

Borrowing

This chapter introduces the concept of borrowing for consumers. Borrowing is about using other people's money for meeting current requirements for which you do not have enough of your own money. The lender, usually an institution like a bank, lends money on the strength of their evaluation of the borrower's repayment capacity. Borrowing by individuals for various purposes, like the acquisition of assets, has become increasingly popular over the last few decades. They no longer want to wait till they collect enough money, usually in the later part of their lives, to fulfill their desires.

The topics covered in this chapter are:

- Introduction to borrowing
- Credit risk
- Consumer reporting agencies
- Consumer reporting applications

- Credit scores

- Consumer credit report applications

- Why you should check consumer reports

- Types of borrowing

5.1 Introduction to Borrowing

Borrowing is using money that you currently do not have.

While working on borrowed funds has been a feature of how businesses operate, for individuals, traditional wisdom has called for earning and saving money before spending it. However, that invariably meant a life of hardship spent working and saving money and not being able to enjoy the fruits of one's labor till no longer young.

When you borrow, you buy financial resources or capital. It is a purchase because there is a cost attached to it – that of interest. With the help of financial resources so created, you come into a position of purchasing and owning assets that you would otherwise not have been in a position to. This ability of borrowing, or credit, to fulfill desires and aspirations, has made it increasingly popular over the last century, even as the middle class and economic prosperity increased in America.

Borrowing is also referred to as "credit." When you buy something without paying for it, you are buying it on credit. "Credit" derives from the Latin word credere (to believe).

It has several meanings as a verb in common usage – to recognize with respect, to acknowledge a contribution – but in finance, it generally means to allow delayed payment. Both credit and debt are forms of borrowing.

Snippets from "Credit History: The Evolution of Consumer Credit in America" by the Federal Reserve Bank of Boston[10]

"Everything came together in the 1920s.

Auto manufacturers perfected assembly line production and began to turn out cars at a price that would 'put the middle class on wheels.' Public investment in a federal highway system helped to expand the market even further. Other manufacturers adapted assembly line techniques to produce affordable home appliances and consumer electronics: ovens, refrigerators, washing machines, phonographs, radios, telephones."

"But the catalyst – the thing that helped to bring all these industrial and technological marvels within the reach of so many consumers – was the expanded use of installment credit. The big breakthrough came in 1919 when General Motors Acceptance Corporation (GMAC) became the first to make financing available to middle-income car buyers. Instead of having to come up with the entire purchase price, prospective car buyers needed only a down payment and an income that was big enough to cover monthly payments over the life of the loan. Before long, manufacturers of other 'big ticket' items began to adopt the practice. And if consumers were hesitant to

---

10. www.bostonfed.org. "Credit History: The Evolution of Consumer Credit in America." Accessed September 29, 2023. https://www.bostonfed.org/-/media/Documents/ledger/spring-summer2004/credhistory.pdf.

go into debt, the flood of advertisements in mass media outlets – newspapers, magazines, and radio – helped them to overcome their inhibitions."

"The use of consumer credit had become a fixture of everyday life. In 2000, more than 70 percent of US households had at least one general-purpose credit card...Thirty years earlier, in 1970, the number was only 16 percent. After the 1920s there was no turning back. Widespread use of consumer credit became an indispensable part of American economic life."

"Credit cards as we know them today didn't take off until the 1960s when financial innovation, improved technology, and changing consumer attitudes all converged."

Milton Friedman's 1980s book, "Free to Choose,"[11] reflected the growing financial freedom for consumers, including marginalized sections.

5.2 Credit Risk

A borrower needs a lender. Without a lender, there is no borrower.

Why would a lender lend money to a borrower? After all, it is a risky transaction. What happens if the borrower is unable to repay the debt? What happens if the asset for which the money was borrowed, and on which the lender has a right in case of default, is not available or recoverable?

---

11. Milton Friedman, Free to Choose: A Personal Statement (New York, 1980)

One answer to the question is that lenders lend money because the money they have is a resource and they need to put it to use. As we have seen in an earlier chapter, money has a time value. Its capacity to purchase reduces over time. If the lender does not put his money to use, he will be gradually able to buy less and less with it. Lending it enables him to earn from it and stay ahead of the curve on which money loses value over time.

The other answer lies in the process of credit risk assessment through which a lender establishes the borrower's ability, capacity, and intent of paying back the money borrowed. When credit was not common, and offered only to people known well, the credit evaluation process was implicit in the agreement to lend money (or not). The lender would not lend money unless reasonably confident of the borrower's ability to repay. This judgment would be made based on his knowledge of the borrower.

5.3 Consumer Reporting Agencies

With credit taking off in the last century, and millions of people beginning to purchase on credit, including people unknown to the lender or the seller, individual evaluation of each person became an onerous and expensive task.

This brought into the picture credit rating agencies, private companies whose business was to track individual lives, events therein, and transactions that could have a bearing on their ability to repay borrowed sums of money.

While there were many such agencies to begin with, over time, as access to nationwide information has become easier, they have consolidated into three agencies which are:

- Experian

- Equifax

- TransUnion

Their primary role is to maintain information about consumers that could impact their creditworthiness, or ability to borrow and repay. They track:

- Payment history

- Amounts owed by you

- Credit history length

- New credit applications open

- Types of credit received (car loan, credit card, etc.)

Consumer reports issued by these three agencies have wide applications that extend beyond credit evaluation. This data could be used:

- By lenders who may be considering offering you credit

- By lenders when you apply for enhancement of credit limits

- By lenders who wish to qualify you for offers

- By employers who are considering you for employment

- By landlords considering a tenancy arrangement with you

- By utility companies

- For background check for any purpose
- By yourself for checking scores and report contents

The data is released only if authorized by you.

5.4 Credit Score

A credit score is a number that summarizes your standing as a borrower. It could also determine the rates at which money is offered to you.

The consumer reporting agency does not issue a credit score. It provides information about the consumer based on which the buyer of the report can reach a decision. Thus, an individual could have many credit scores arising out of different scoring models used by the evaluators.

There are two companies that issue scores that have come to be used as standard scoring models without the need for the buyer/user to generate their own. These are:

5.4.1 FICO score

This was introduced by the Fair Isaac Corp. in 1989 and is claimed to be used by 90% of lenders. It has been used almost interchangeably with "credit score." There are multiple versions of FICO scores, meant for different purposes and for different users.

5.4.2 VantageScore

The three consumer information agencies have collaborated to produce VantageScore, which is understood to be gaining acceptance with users. The similarities between the two scores are:

- Both assign higher scores for good credit and lower scores for poor credit.

- The score ranges from 300 to 850 in both.

5.5 Why Should You Check Your Credit Report?

As a credit report pertains to you, it is in your interest to ensure that the data reported by the agencies is accurate. Inaccurate reports could impair your ability to raise credit when you need it the most.

You are entitled to a free report annually from each of the three agencies. As there could be differences in the information maintained by each of them, asking all of them for a report is advised.

It is easy. You can request a report through www.annualcreditreport.com. Making sure your credit report is accurate results in an accurate credit score as well.

Tips for building a strong credit score from the Consumer Financial Protection Bureau (CFPB)[12], a US government agency that makes sure banks, lenders, and other financial companies treat consumers fairly.

Pay loans on time. If required, set up reminders and alarm systems as well as automated payment instructions. But do not default.

Do not take all the credit you are eligible for. Most credit scoring models will interpret this as a sign that you are not desperate for more credit. If you are close to maxing out on a credit card, a strategy could be to get an additional card but not use its limit. Thus, your limit goes up but usage does not, making it a smaller percentage of the available limit. 30% of the limit is a ballpark number recommended by some experts.

The longer your demonstration of creditworthy behavior, the better the credit score. Fight the desire to splurge and undo the good work of the past. It means you will need to start afresh. A much saner way is to build on the good work of the past.

If you don't need that loan, why apply for it? Bunched-up credit-seeking activity indicates a worsening of the financial situation. It can only mean bad news for your credit score.

Fact check your credit. It has nothing to do with spending or receiving money. All you need to ensure is that the date these agencies are working with is accurate and shows you in the best possible light.

---

12. "How do I get and keep a good credit score," Consumer Education, Consumer Financial Protection Bureau, updated September 01, 2020

Make use of products such as secured credit cards that have been designed to help people build and improve their credit scores. Otherwise, you could end up in a Catch-22 situation. You cannot get credit because you don't have a good credit score and you cannot improve your score because you are unable to get credit.

5.6 Types of Borrowing

While there are many ways of classifying loans, as consumers, we understand them best as products or product types. The most popular ones are:

5.6.1 Housing loan or home loan or mortgage loan

Home loans are widely used across the nation. They either support the purchase of a home or the taking of a loan against equity in an existing home. Home Loans are covered in detail in the next chapter on home ownership.

5.6.2 Vehicle loan or auto loan

Vehicle loans are another popular lending product and widely accessible considering that the lender has the security of an asset, the vehicle, to secure them against non-payment by the borrower.

However, unlike a home, a vehicle is a depreciating asset that starts reducing rapidly in value the moment it is taken out of the showroom. Hence, lenders may not be willing to advance the full amount needed, to provide for the reduction in value.

Auto loans are usually offered with repayment periods ranging between two and seven years.

5.6.3 Student loan

The Department of Education makes most of the student loans in the US. Many students and families also rely on private student loans to either get funding when they are not eligible for federal loans or to get additional financing to cover costs not covered by the federal loans.

Considering that repayment usually starts several years after the loan is taken, they are fraught with non-payment risks. They assume a repayment capacity in the future that may not materialize.

The standard repayment period for federal loans is 10 years while private ones do not have any specific standard. A federal loan does not require a credit score for qualification. Repayment is triggered when certain conditions are satisfied, with the key one being that of six months after graduation.

5.6.4 Personal loan

While mortgage loans, auto loans, and student loans are also personal loans, they are referred to by their own product name, possibly because they are widely used and have become products; common minimum terms and conditions have evolved for their grant.

There are several other types of personal loans that depend on individual needs and situations and are dependent on the borrower and lender for the determination of its terms and conditions. Some are:

- Wedding loan

- Loan for a medical emergency

- Vacation loan

5.6.5 Payday loan

A payday loan makes available the money a salaried person is going to receive, a few days before it is due. While it may be made on the basis of an urgent need professed by the borrower, the lender's interest generally is to charge high rates of interest for the few days the money is borrowed. While it may be a necessity when taken, it is usually detrimental to the finances of the borrower as he is required to pay a high cost in the form of interest. Hence, prospective borrowers are advised to consider alternatives before going in for a payday loan.

5.6.6 Pawn shop loan

This is one of the more traditional forms of borrowing. You take an item of value to a pawn shop which, if satisfied, will advance a certain percentage of the assessed value of the product. Generally, items like personal jewelry or expensive electronic items are used for this purpose as they hold substantial value. When the money, along with interest charges, is returned, the item pawned is retrieved.

5.6.7 Credit card

Ever since their introduction, credit cards have continued to gain in popularity and revolutionized consumer borrowing.

A cardholder needs to undergo a credit evaluation only once, at the time a card is issued, and thereafter continue to run up a bill against the credit limit established. It makes cards extremely flexible and easy to use. In fact, their ease of use has sometimes earned criticism as being responsible for overspending by cardholders.

The other major benefit of credit cards is that the consumer does not pay interest on the amount used, as long as he pays the periodic bill in a timely manner. On the flip side, in case you do not square off by the required date, and choose to revolve the credit, credit cards levy high rates of interest.

5.7 Protection and Safeguards for Borrowers

Borrowers should make an effort to arm themselves with knowledge about the safeguards available to them so that they can act in case of unfair treatment by lenders. Some of the main ones are:

Consumer Financial Protection Bureau (CFPB): The CFPB is a government agency responsible for enforcing consumer protection laws related to financial products and services, including loans.

Fair Debt Collection Practices Act (FDCPA)[13]**:** The FDCPA regulates and prohibits collectors of debt from engaging in abusive, deceptive, or unfair practices when collecting debts.

Fair Credit Reporting Act (FCRA)[14]**:** Credit reporting agencies are required to maintain accurate and up-to-date information on borrowers, and provide an opportunity for borrowers to review and dispute any errors or inaccuracies in their credit reports.

Truth in Lending Act (TILA)[15]**:** Lenders are required to disclose in writing the terms and conditions of a loan, such as fees and interest rates, including the annual percentage rate. Advertisements are also required to contain certain disclosures. This allows borrowers to make an informed decision before taking out a loan.

State-level protections: In addition to these federal laws, many states have additional protection for borrowers that seek to ensure that they are not victimized, including the requirement for lenders to offer alternative repayment plans to borrowers finding it difficult to repay on original terms.

---

13. "Fair Debt Collection Practices Act," Federal Trade Commission, https://www.ftc. gov/legal-library/browse/rules/fair-debt-collection-practices-act-text, accessed August 2, 2023

14. "Fair Credit Reporting Act," Federal Trade Commission, https://www.ftc.gov/legal-library/browse/statutes/fair-credit-reporting-act, accessed August 2, 2023

15. "Truth in Lending Act," Federal Trade Commission, https://www.ftc.gov/legal-library/browse/statutes/truth-lending-act, accessed August 2, 2023

Quiz

1. **Agreed use of money that you do not have is known as?**

   a. Borrowing

   b. Lending

   c. Cash Flow

   d. Income

2. **Borrowing is known as the purchase of capital because** _____

   a. you generally purchase assets with the borrowed money.

   b. you pay a cost for it in the form of interest.

   c. businesses borrow money and they regularly do sales and purchase of goods.

   d. None of the above

3. **Without access to borrowing money, most people are likely to be able to** _____

   a. sell assets much later in life.

   b. earn income much earlier in life.

   c. earn income much later in life.

   d. buy assets much later in life.

4. **Which of the following terms can be used in place of borrowing? (Select all applicable).**

    a. Liability

    b. Asset

    c. Credit

    d. Advance

5. **What most significantly influenced widespread access to the many technological marvels developed in the twentieth century was _____.**

    a. the assembly line

    b. availability of installment credit

    c. expansion of the middle-class

    d. the federal highway network

6. **Credit risk refers to _____**

    a. the borrower not being able to obtain the loan he seeks.

    b. interest rate on a loan being very high.

    c. the borrower not being able to pay back the loan he has taken.

    d. taking a loan but not spending it in the way it was originally intended.

7. **Lenders are agreeable to taking credit risk because? (Select all applicable)**

   a. Money sitting idle loses value

   b. They can earn interest on it

   c. They can always sell off the asset purchased with borrowed money and make a recovery

   d. Borrowers are their friends and cannot default on repayment

8. **Select the names that are one of the three main consumer reporting agencies.**

   a. FICO

   b. Vantage

   c. Experian

   d. Federal Reserve

9. **TransUnion operates _____.**

   a. nationally

   b. in a few states in the South

   c. in a few states on the West Coast

   d. only in New York and New Jersey

10. **Consumer reporting agencies are legally required to share their consumer-specific information with consumers every _____.**

    a. month

    b. quarter

    c. six months

    d. year

Answers	1 – a	2 – b	3 – d	4 – c, d	5 – b
	6 – c	7 – a, b	8 – c	9 – a	10 – d

Chapter Summary

◆ In this chapter, we introduced the concept of borrowing by consumers and discussed various aspects related to it.

◆ Consumer reporting agencies track the credit history of individuals with the help of various data points. Lenders can access this data, usually for a fee, as an aid to their credit evaluation process.

◆ There are other agencies that issue credit scores for individuals based on the tracked data.

◆ Consumers can borrow money for various reasons, such as buying a house, buying a car, financing education, and many others. Payday and Pawnshop loans are other types of consumer borrowings.

◆ Credit cards are a popular borrowing mechanism.

This page is intentionally left blank

Chapter 6

Home Ownership

A place one can call home is one of the most basic needs of human beings, perhaps all creatures. Home can be a shelter, a sanctuary, or a place one keeps coming back to. It is a supporting, protective environment that enables us to be us.

According to Robert Rubinstein, who has taught anthropology at the University of Maryland at Baltimore County, "American culture is strongly rooted in feelings of independence, autonomy, and control. We live in a society that is concerned with freedom, and part of that development is being able to make a space for yourself, and having a central place from which to look out at the world."

This chapter introduces home ownership and various aspects related to it:

- The importance of a home
- Buy or rent

- Mortgage loans

- Types of mortgage loans

- The mortgage loan process

- Mortgage calculator

- Factors affecting interest rate

6.1 The Importance of a Home

With the comfort of familiar surroundings, known people in the neighborhood, and a sense of belonging from which emanates our identity, home is a central part of being who we are.

The phrase "home is where the heart is," attributed to Gaius Plinius Secundus, a Roman naval commander, perhaps captures the sentiment of a home well.

From a financial perspective, a home is just another asset that needs to be a part of our plans. However, in view of its importance to the lives of Americans, a separate chapter has been devoted to it.

6.2 Buy or Rent

While having a home is an essential requirement, buying a home may not be. Renting one is a popular choice as well.

St. Louis FED tracks home ownership and rentership based on US Census Bureau data.

Table 6.1

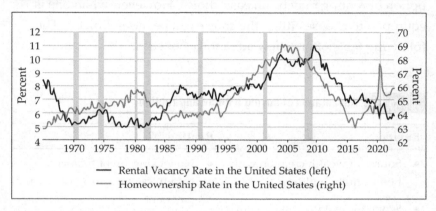

— Rental Vacancy Rate in the United States (left)
— Homeownership Rate in the United States (right)

Note: Shaded area indicate U.S. recessions.
Source: US Census Bureau

From 1965 through 2022:

- Home ownership went from 63% in 1965 to 66% in 2022, after scaling a peak of 69% in 2005. The balance is renters.

- Vacant rental properties, used as a measure of the popularity of renting, have gone from 8.5% in 1965 to 6% in 2022, after scaling a peak of 11% in 2011.

The choice between renting and ownership generally follows a life-cycle pattern. Young adults are more likely to rent as their financial resources are limited, and they perhaps also put a premium on mobility and have low attachments and responsibilities. As young families take shape and income increases, the desire to own a home, and build equity becomes stronger, leading to a greater level of home ownership. Sunset years, with fewer responsibilities and smaller families, may lead to downsizing the home to an owned apartment, or even a rented one.

When the financial situation does not permit a purchase, the option of renting may be an easy choice. However, when one is equipped to choose either, the choice can be more difficult. The following table offers a few advantages of each.

Table 6.1	Advantages of buying a home and renting
Buying	**Renting**
• Source of wealth creation with home equity build-up	• No locking-up of financial resources in the form of down payment
• Scope for making a statement about personal lifestyle and choices; can build or equip it based on one's own choices	• Major maintenance is the landlord's responsibility
• Benefit of tax deductions available on mortgage interest payment	• Flexibility of mobility without worrying about the property
• Predictable long-term installment expense with an agreed payment plan	• Easy to start

6.3 Mortgage Loans

Mortgage loans are designed to facilitate the purchase of property. According to the Consumer Financial Protection

Bureau[16], "mortgage loans are used to buy a home or to borrow money against the value of a home you already own."

Mortgage loans derive their name from mortgage, a legal term for "an agreement between you and a lender that gives the lender the right to take your property if you fail to repay the money you've borrowed plus interest," as also defined by the Consumer Financial Protection Bureau. Similarly, mortgage loan borrowing conditions provide for the lender to repossess the property against the security for which the loan was granted in order to recover outstanding dues in case of default in payment by the borrower.

A home is the single biggest item of purchase and a mortgage loan is the single biggest financial responsibility most of us will assume over a lifetime. Hence, all aspects related to the purchase of a home on the basis of a mortgage loan assume importance for the buyer/borrower.

The Federal Reserve Bank of New York Center for Microeconomic Data[17] demonstrates the primacy of mortgage debt (including HELOC) in the consumer debt pie, accounting for over 70% of the outstanding balances.

16. "What is a mortgage," Consumer Financial Protection Bureau, last reviewed February 22, 2022, https://www.consumerfinance.gov/ask-cfpb/what-is-a-mortgage-en-99/#:~:text=A%20mortgage%20is%20an%20agreement,a%20home%20you%20already%20own

17. "Press Release," Federal Reserve Bank of New York, dated February 16, 2023, https://www.newyorkfed.org/newsevents/news/research/2023/20230216

| Figure 6.2 | Household Debt as of Q4 2022 |

Consumer debt by type ($ trillion)

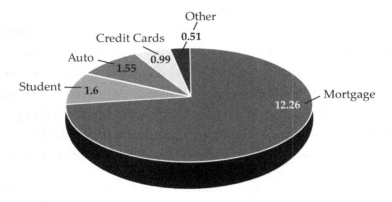

6.4 Types of Mortgage Loans

There are several types of mortgage loans one can choose from. Hence, in order to make the right choice, one must know about them.

6.4.1 Conventional mortgage

This is the standard mortgage loan, not backed by any government agency. Everybody is eligible, but eligibility norms are usually stringent. As they operate in a competitive market, the terms they offer, such as the rate of interest, could sometimes be favorable for borrowers. The borrower may also be free to choose the period of repayment.

These loans could trigger an additional cost for the borrower in the form of paying for private mortgage insurance (PMI) if the down payment is under 20% or till the outstanding loan balance comes to under 80% of the property value. This seeks to protect the lender against the erosion of value in case they need to repossess and sell.

6.4.2 Government-backed loans

The US government insures or guarantees certain types of mortgage loans, making it easier for both borrowers and lenders. The common ones are:

Federal Housing Administration (FHA) loans

These are insured by the FHA and designed to make mortgage borrowing simpler for people with modest incomes and lower credit scores, and permit low down payments.

US Department of Agriculture (USDA) loans

These loans are designed to make it easier to buy property in rural areas. They usually have a zero down payment and lower closing costs. Moreover, the geographical area covered is quite wide and often includes neighborhoods one might not consider rural.

Veterans (VA) loans

These are offered to retired as well as active US military personnel. The Department of Veterans Affairs (VA) guarantees these loans which are generally easy to qualify for by target beneficiaries. These loans carry benefits like zero down payment, lower closing cost, and no mortgage insurance regardless of outstanding value being less than 80% or not.

6.4.3 Fixed-rate loan

As the name suggests, the rate of interest is defined at the time of origination and remains fixed for the life of the loan.

6.4.4 Adjustable-rate loan

Also known as a variable-rate mortgage, this loan carries a variable rate of interest that is defined as a certain number of percentage points over the bank rate. Even in these loans, the first few years carry a fixed rate after which they change to the variable interest rate mechanism.

6.4.5 Home Equity Line of Credit (HELOC)

HELOC is a credit facility that can be taken against the equity of your home. If the home is debt-free, then the entire value of the home is your equity against which a loan can be taken. If the home was purchased on a mortgage loan, the equity you have in your home is that part of your home that is no longer required as security for the lender. In other words, you have already repaid some part of the loan.

HELOC is issued in the form of a line of credit which can be reused as you repay the part that was borrowed earlier, much like a credit card. It could be useful for big-ticket purchases.

6.4.6 Home Equity Loan

A Home Equity loan is similar to a HELOC as it is taken against the equity in your home. It is a more traditional loan that needs to be paid back in the form of installments over an agreed period of time.

6.4.7 Reverse mortgage

A reverse mortgage enables the conversion of home equity into money without the need to sell it off or take an additional repayment burden. The repayment of this loan needs to be done at the time of vacating the home permanently. It could also be upon the death of the borrowers.

The loan is called a reverse mortgage because instead of making monthly payments to a lender, as is done with a traditional mortgage, in this case, the lender makes payments to the borrower, usually monthly.

It must be noted that the loan types described above are not mutually exclusive. Combinations are possible. For example, a conventional mortgage can be either a fixed-rate loan or an adjustable-rate loan. Similarly, a VA loan can be either a fixed-rate or adjustable-rate loan.

Based on data provided by the US Census Bureau, Mortgage News Daily[18] broke down home purchases by the type of finance used.

18. "New Houses by Type of Financing," Housing Data, Mortgage News Daily, accessed on August 2, 2023, https://www.mortgagenewsdaily.com/data/financing-type

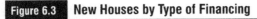

Figure 6.3   **New Houses by Type of Financing**

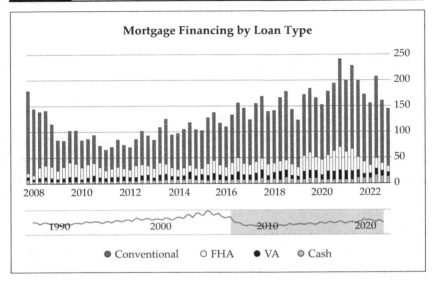

Note: New Houses by Type of Financing data is published quarterly by the US Bureau of Census. The units displayed are in thousands of homes/ structures.

Historically, conventional mortgage loans have accounted for over 70% of home sales, except for a brief duration after the 2008 mortgage-triggered financial crisis. If we add other types of financing, over 90% of home sales have been on the basis of one type of financing or another.

6.5 The Mortgage Loan Process

A mortgage loan is a significant commitment, both for the buyer as well as the lender. While for a lender it is a business, and they will likely have specialists handling it, for a borrower it is usually a first-time experience and can be overwhelming. Hence, an understanding of the requirements will, hopefully, help you navigate it with greater ease.

6.5.1 What you should do before applying for a loan

Identify the property

This, of course, is the obvious starting point. That being said, it is normally completed only after the "preapproval" of the loan has been done.

Check your credit

Lenders will want to ensure that you are in a position to repay the loan and interest before lending the money. One of the key elements in that decision is the report they receive from one of the three consumer reporting agencies and the credit score, either calculated by them based on their own algorithm or sourced from an external agency.

It would be a good idea to ensure that your credit score meets the minimum criteria set by the identified lender. There is no value in applying and being rejected, at least for obvious reasons. If the report highlights areas that can be fixed, it is a good idea to fix them first before seeking a loan.

Collect information on loan types

There are many types of loans available, some with better terms than others. Read more about them in the section on "Types of Mortgage Loans."

Shop for a suitable lender

Check out rates and conditions offered by lenders and shortlist one or two. Mortgage loans are offered by a variety of lenders. In addition, each state has a housing finance agency that works with lenders and borrowers.

6.5.2 Processing with the lender

The formal part begins once you approach a lender for a loan.

Pre approval

This is an initial verification by the lender of your creditworthiness based on the documents you have submitted and what your credit score says.

This is not a commitment but an indication of the willingness to lend subject to the underwriting requirements being satisfied and there being no substantial change in your circumstances between now and the closure.

Finalize the property and make an offer

Armed with the preapproval, you can now finalize the property and make an offer. This might require paying upfront "earnest" money. This money is counted towards the down payment when the loan is finally granted.

Complete the formal application for the loan

Having made an offer, possibly with money, now is the time to get moving towards the final loan approval. This will require completing the loan application forms and providing data regarding your financials which would include, among other things, information on:

- Assets and liabilities
- Income and expenses
- Availability of funds for down payment
- Details of property
- Work-related history

A loan estimate will be issued by the lender which will detail the various costs for you. This is issued usually within three days of submitting your application.

Processing and underwriting

The lender works with the information you have submitted in an effort to evaluate your creditworthiness and the cost that needs to be levied in the form of an interest rate.

There could be some back and forth between you and the lender for more information and clarifications. This is the stage at which the interest rate will be agreed and locked.

Fun fact:

Home inspection could help lower your acquisition cost.

The underwriter usually asks for a home inspection. It is meant to protect the lender, as well as you, by ensuring that it is worth what you have agreed to pay. It happens by comparing the prices of homes that could be considered similar.

In some cases, a lower evaluation could help you in negotiating the price downwards with the seller.

Closing

Eventually, you will receive a letter of commitment. If you are agreeable with the terms offered, the closure will happen which will require you to make commitments by signing the required documents. You will agree to the terms of the transfer of your property. You will need to pay the fees that have been advised earlier. You will also need to submit the down payment. And the home is yours.

The Consumer Financial Protection Bureau[19] advises the seven things to look for in a mortgage:

- The size of the loan

- The interest rate and any associated points

- The closing costs of the loan, including the lender's fees

- The Annual Percentage Rate (APR)

- The type of interest rate and whether it can change (is it fixed or adjustable?)

- The loan term, or how long you have to repay the loan

- Whether the loan has other risky features, such as a prepayment penalty, a balloon clause, an interest-only feature, or negative amortization

---

19. "Seven things to look for in a mortgage," What is a Mortgage, Consumer Financial Protection Bureau, last reviewed February 22, 2022, https://www.consumerfinance.gov/ask-cfpb/what-is-a-mortgage-en-99/#:~:text=A%20 mortgage%20is%20an%20 argument,a%20home%20you%20already%20own

6.6 Mortgage Calculator

A fixed-rate mortgage is structured as an annuity which requires periodic payments of equal amounts. A part goes towards interest and another towards principal repayment. In the early years, the larger part goes towards interest repayment but the situation reverses as the loan progresses.

Though monthly repayment requirements can be calculated based on the terms, for ease of borrowers, and for enabling them to estimate repayment requirements, there are many calculators available on mortgage-related websites where borrowers can find out an approximate figure.

6.6.1 Mortgage factor

Monthly mortgage payments can be estimated using the mortgage factor. The mortgage factor is a calculation of the payment per $1,000 of the mortgage loan, given the interest rate and the maturity of the mortgage. These are ready tables made available by a variety of resources. The table below shows factors for 15, 20, and 30-year loans at different rates of interest:

Table 6.2 **Mortgage factor calculator**

Amount of loan	Rate of interest	15 years	20 years	30 years
1,000	4.00	7.40	6.06	4.77
1,000	4.50	7.65	6.33	5.07
1,000	5.00	7.91	6.60	5.37
1,000	5.50	8.17	6.88	5.68
1,000	6.00	8.44	7.16	6.00

What this means is that if your loan amount to be repaid is $1,000 and the interest rate 6%, for a 15-year loan the monthly payment required is $8.44 per month. Over 15 years, the borrower would have paid a total of $1,519.20.

So, if you were considering a transaction with the following details:

Home value	$500,000
Down payment	$100,000
Amount financed	$400,000
Loan duration	30 years
Loan type	Fixed rate
Interest rate	5%

The monthly payment will be:

5.37 (the factor for a 30-year loan a 5%) X $400,000 (the amount of loan) ÷ 1,000 (the value at which the factor was calculated)

= $2,148 per month.

6.7 Factors Affecting Interest Rate

Thumb rules for interest rates as per the Consumer Financial Protection Bureau are:

6.7.1 Credit score

The higher the score the lower the interest rate.

6.7.2 Home location

Location of the home could have a bearing on the rate.

6.7.3 Amount of loan

Particularly large or small amounts could attract higher rates.

6.7.4 Down payment

The larger the down payment, the lower the interest rate.

6.7.5 Loan term

The lower the term, the lower the rate.

6.7.6 Loan-type

Government-insured loans like VA and FHA could mean lower rates for eligible people who may have to pay higher rates on conventional loans.

Consumer Financial Protection Bureau makes available a tool that can guide homebuyers on what interest rate to expect. It can be accessed at: www.consumerfinance.gov

Quiz

1. A home is called a home when:

   a. It is owned by the family living in it

   b. It is rented by the family living in it

   c. A family lives in it regardless of ownership

   d. None of the above

2. If vacant rental properties have reduced from 8.5% in 1965 to 6% in 2022, which of the following would be the most definite deduction?

   a. A higher percentage of properties available for rent have been rented in 2022.

   b. A lower percentage of properties available for rent have been rented in 2022.

   c. A higher percentage of people now live in owned properties.

   d. A lower percentage of people now live in owned properties.

3. **The likelihood of renting a home is expected to be highest for?**

   a. Young adults, starting out working and being independent

   b. Middle-aged people around 40, with growing families and income

   c. Retirees

   d. Phase of life does not matter; it is the same for all

4. **There is a greater possibility of wealth creation in _____.**

   a. renting a home

   b. buying a home

   c. both are the same; it depends on the individual

5. **A disadvantage of home buying is that substantial financial resources get locked up in it.**

   a. Agree

   b. Disagree

6. **Mortgage loans derive their name from mortify, which is a legal term for "causing someone to feel ashamed or embarrassed."**

   a. Agree

   b. Disagree

7. **The total debt arising from which of the following constitutes the biggest number (in $ value terms) in the US?**

    a. Credit cards

    b. Student loans

    c. Auto loans

    d. Mortgage loans

8. **Historically, the highest percentage of home sale transactions have happened through financing by:**

    a. Cash

    b. VA loans

    c. Conventional mortgage

    d. Home equity loans

9. **Which of the following types of loan is granted as a revolving line of credit?**

    a. Conventional mortgage

    b. HELOC

    c. Home equity loan

    d. All of the above

10. **Government-backed home loans are issued only as fixed-rate loans.**

   a. Agree

   b. Disagree

Answers	1 – c	2 – a	3 – a	4 – b	5 – a
	6 – b	7 – d	8 – c	9 – b	10 – b

Chapter Summary

◆ In this chapter we introduced the concept of borrowing by consumers and discussed various aspects related to it.

◆ A home has a special meaning for every individual.

◆ An important decision many people need to take is whether to buy or rent a home.

◆ Mortgage Loans, which enable people to buy homes, and also refinance them, come in various types, such as conventional loans, government-backed loans, fixed-rate loans, adjustable-rate loans, Home Equity Line of Credit (HELOC), and reverse mortgages.

◆ The mortgage loan process has many steps. Interested borrowers would do well to prepare themselves by gathering information on the choices so that they eventually sign up for the most suitable form of loan.

◆ The loan terms, like interest rate, can depend on many factors such as the credit score, home location, loan amount, down payment, loan term, and even the loan type.

Chapter **7**

Investing

With the collection of money having become an end in itself, it stands to reason that opportunities would emerge to enable the gatherers to put it to best use. This is what investing is all about, putting away your excess money in a manner that it earns the most while creating the lowest risk. Of course, the risk and return tradeoff is based on personal preferences, but, fundamentally, everyone wants to earn the most at the lowest risk.

This chapter introduces the fundamentals of investing and various aspects related to it such as:

- Introduction to investing

- Investing fundamentals

- Common investment avenues

7.1 Introduction to Investing

Money is the lifeblood running through all spheres of activity in the modern world. It may have been invented, among other reasons, as a common currency to facilitate transactions between human beings, but its relevance has since grown far beyond that early use. The acquisition, accumulation, preservation, and growth of money has become an important goal for most people.

Where does investing fit into the scheme of things?

Investing could be defined as covering the last two of the four goals related to money listed above; that is, its preservation and growth. Investing is how you put money to work in order to have more of it at a later point in time. Or, if that were to be considered a goal too ambitious, at the very least, it should allow us the freedom to be able to purchase the same basket of goods and services as it would have, at the beginning of the investment period. This is relevant considering that we live in an inflationary world, where prices tend to rise over time.

While on the one hand, there is a need to make your money work so that it gives you a return, or money earned from your money, on the other there are a plethora of avenues seeking your investment and promising various benefits, of which a good return is usually one. Bank deposit or stock? Stock or bond? Bond or gold? Gold or property? Property or mutual fund? These are some questions investors must find answers to in their respective investment journeys.

Through wise investing, we seek to make our future more secure in financial terms.

7.2 Investing Fundamentals

7.2.1 There is always some risk

Preservation and growth of money, simple as it may sound, is not an easy task. While one may have needed to protect one's money from being stolen or robbed in the olden days, in the modern world, there are probably even easier ways of losing money.

Making a wrong investment choice is clearly one easy way of losing money. Since one does not know what will happen in the future, sometimes investors continue to hold on in the hope of recovery but end up watching helplessly as the slide continues.

But stocks are a known risky investment. What about investments sold as risk-free, or low-risk?

Nothing is risk-free. Even the safest investment carries an element of risk. Investing is a choice made by the investor. A choice needs to be made because the future is uncertain.

Though we have some idea about how it might turn out, based on the general principles of life in a civil society that have evolved over time, nobody knows for sure. Just because a certain commodity has appreciated over the last five years does not mean it will do so for the next five years as well. Investment advertisements regularly and mandatorily warn investors that past performance is no guarantee of future returns.

What you are not explicitly told is that there is risk in every investment. Bank deposits carry the risk of bank failure. Deposits in banks are insured up to a defined value by the Federal Deposit Insurance Corporation or FDIC.

So, where does the FDIC get the money with which it pays depositors? The FDIC is "an independent agency created by Congress to maintain stability and public confidence in the nation's financial system." It collects a premium from insured banks which becomes its corpus for meeting insurance pay-out needs.

> **Fun fact:**
>
> Since the founding of the Federal Deposit Insurance Corporation in 1933, no depositor has lost a penny of FDIC-insured funds.[20]

That the FDIC is "backed by the full faith and credit of the United States government" further adds to its credibility. It becomes a government, or sovereign risk in a way. But there could be other risks.

While a government might ensure that instruments like bank deposits are honored, they cannot guarantee the non-depreciation of the currency in case of economic mismanagement. You may get your $100 back, but if that now buys only half of what it did earlier, it is another type of risk. There could also be liquidity risk; inability to cash out when you need the money.

7.2.2 There is a trade-off between risk and return

Each investor is unique.

---

20. "Understanding Deposit Insurance," FDIC, last updated July 13, 2020, https://www. fdic.gov/resources/deposit-insurance/understanding-deposit-insurance/

Different people find different answers to their investment questions as each individual has a unique set of circumstances that drive his/her choices. This is despite the fact that historical data is available to all in a transparent manner. At the same time, each individual could take a different view of the future. Take stocks for example. Each time someone buys a stock, someone else sells it.

Most investment advisors will have investors fill out a form based on which they evaluate the "risk profile," or ability to take investment risks and recommend options accordingly.

The risk-reward trade-off is well known. The greater the projected return, the greater the risk. If this was not the case, and lower-risk investments yielded better returns, why would anyone choose high-risk and low-return investments?

Many investor choices are driven by a choice of the right place where on the risk and return, or reward, continuum one wishes to be. Investors with a low ability to handle risk are recommended safe options like government bonds and bank deposits, while investors with a greater risk appetite might be recommended riskier options like stocks, which could also deliver higher returns.

What is the risk in investing?

It can be any factor that impairs the prospect of generating expected returns. It could be economic conditions such as inflation, industry-specific concerns such as the travel industry during the pandemic, or company-specific issues like damage to a major production unit. By their very nature, risks are unpredictable. If they were certain, they would be factored into the pricing. Careful decision-making can possibly reduce the impact of risks, but not eliminate them.

Investors should also note that high returns at high risk mean that there will be situations when negative returns are realized. In other words, you lose a part of your principal invested. It does not mean that since you have decided to invest in a riskier instrument, a higher return is guaranteed.

Liquidity need is often the other factor, apart from risk and return, that drives investment choices. Market-beating returns are great, but of no value if the money cannot be availed when most needed. That is also considered a risk in investing.

7.2.3 Diversification of portfolio is desirable

Not putting all of one's eggs in one basket is another one of the most fundamental rules of investing. Recognizing that the future is uncertain, investors need to make investment decisions that consider the fact that their investments may not turn out the way they thought they would at the time of making the investment. This is applicable even to investors who have an appetite for bearing high levels of risk. You do not want freak accidents and events wiping out your future.

You believe you have identified the perfect stock to invest in. You expect it to deliver handsome returns over a long period of time. Now you have a choice. You could invest all your available money into it, or you could invest a part and the remaining in some other stock.

By investing all in that one stock you are giving yourself the best chance of a good return. However, you are also exposing yourself to a high level of risk as it is an individual stock exposed to events, circumstances, cycles, and other vagaries. By not investing the entire amount in this single stock, you are probably going to earn lower returns, but you are protecting yourself against the risk of a total wipe-out in the event of a freak incident derailing that one investment.

Diversification can be done at many levels. You could invest in the stock of another company in the same industry or you could invest in the stock of a company in a different industry, giving you additional protection against a freak incident impacting the original industry.

You could invest the remaining amount in a mutual fund, gaining greater protection with exposure to a basket and not individual funds or you could invest the balance in fixed-income securities such as bonds, gaining further protection against the vagaries of a single market, the stock market.

7.2.4 Investing has a cost – keep it low

Putting money to work is a task. There is a cost involved in investing.

Just like you need to make choices between various investment options available, so do the people and institutions you entrust your money with. They have to put the money to work too so that they are able to generate a return from it and share it with you. If they just sit on the money, it will be a loss-making proposition for them.

Putting money to work involves cost. When you deposit money with a bank, they need to lend it out to companies and individuals who will be charged interest which becomes their return, a part of which gets shared with you based on agreed terms. The cost of this effort is factored into the interest rate promised on the deposit. Even the safety net of FDIC comes at a cost. Member banks pay a fee to be a part of it and get the right to say that they are insured by FDIC.

When you deposit money with a fund, they need to research markets, move money around, and make choices in line with the objective of the fund. Many funds charge a management fee to their investors on an annual basis in order to pay for these costs.

Investors who like to study markets and inform themselves before making investment decisions also invest their time in them. That is a cost. Financial advisors also cost money.

Most individuals have a long investment horizon, from the time they start working, till the time they retire from active work. Annual and other fees over a long horizon become substantial. Hence, keeping the investment cost low can deliver a huge benefit over several decades.

7.2.5 Taxes reduce earnings

"Nothing is certain but death and taxes" goes the proverb.

With some exceptions, most forms of income generated through investments are taxable. Hence, the correct way of evaluating returns from an investment is after accounting for taxation. You may have earned a 10% return, but if you need to pay 30% taxes on the return, what you are left with is only a seven percent return, after taking out 30% of 10 which is three.

Holding on to and maximizing gains requires being tax-aware.

7.2.6 Know your investment horizon

What period of time are you investing your money for? Putting away money for the future is a smart thing to do, but not having it available when you need it, is not.

In the US, the concept of retirement and saving for retirement gained traction in the 1930s with the introduction of social security. While there is no single retirement age, 65, when social security payments could be encashed, has been considered as that number.

In 1900, the 65+ group had only three million members, reflecting a nation with a young population, a mere four percent in a population size of 76 million. Life expectancy crossed 65 in 1944. Therefore, till 1944, the probability of the retired adult enjoying the fruits of his savings was low, since the average person did not live beyond 65. It crossed 70 in 1964. Even in 1964, only five years of post-retirement expenses were needed by most people. Creating a fund over 40 years of working life for a retirement period of five years did not create too many cases of distress.

However, with rising life expectancy, it is close to 80 now, the requirement has kept increasing, along with which has gone up the need to save a larger part of earnings during working years. It helps to be realistic while projecting your investment horizon and liquidity needs.

7.3 Common Financial Investment Avenues

Bank deposit or stock? Stock or bond? Bond or gold? Gold or property? Property or mutual fund? So many choices and so little time, or money.

As a liquid resource, money can be used and invested in many ways. A short-term loan of $1,000 to a friend in need who promises to pay back with an additional $50 as interest, is also an investment. You hope to earn from your money. But it is a private transaction that is not captured in any data or report. It is difficult to determine the volume and outcome of these investments.

Expensive works of art are another form of investment. Each piece is unique with the transaction being at a negotiated price. One Van Gogh is different from another. A Van Gogh is different from a Raphael. It is worth as much or as little as what an investor is willing to pay for it. No more and no less.

What we will cover here are the common investment avenues that are available to everyone and governed by rules and regulations designed to prevent misuse and promote transparency.

7.3.1 Bank accounts

Almost everyone has a bank account. We need bank accounts for carrying out financial transactions, keeping money safe, and making and receiving payments. The returns are low, but the money is secure, if you ensure compliance with FDIC rules.

Savings account

You can keep money in this account and use it for transactions. The balance in the account earns you interest. The rate of interest is low but the money is available when you need it.

A variant of the traditional savings account has emerged in the form of a high-yield online savings account. These typically permit online-only transactions but are able to offer better rates as the bank saves money on physical facilities.

Certificate of deposit (CD)

A CD is money that you deposit in a bank for a defined period of time. Premature withdrawal, if permitted, could entail some financial penalties. In return for the assurance of the money being available to them, banks are able to offer better rates.

7.3.2 Mutual fund (MF)

A mutual fund collects assets together from many investors and manages the pooled corpus in a transparent, professional manner that individuals themselves may not be in a position to do.

Mutual funds could be of a wide variety. Some could be focused on stocks while some may focus on bonds. There could be industry-specific funds and there could be index-based funds. There could also be special-purpose funds such as an ESG fund that raises money to invest in the ESG ecosystem.

Actively-managed funds might levy a higher management fee while funds that track a certain index, say the S&P 500, may levy lower fees as their investments are driven by the index composition.

Mutual funds are a great way to diversify asset allocation. Funds will typically, as part of their own management principles, spread their investments out, within the defined parameters.

7.3.3 Exchange-traded fund (ETF)

In essence, ETFs are the same as mutual funds, being a pooled collection of assets, for transparent and professional management for better returns to participants.

The main difference is that ETFs can be traded through an exchange in much the same way a stock can be. This delivers greater transparency to the pricing, as it is market-determined. Moreover, investors control the investment more closely, as they are able to buy and sell at any time.

Being exchange-traded, ETFs can usually be bought and sold in much smaller quantities than MFs. This gives even small investors a chance to own ETFs.

7.3.4 Company stock

Ever since the emergence of the joint stock corporation, it has been a vehicle for growth in many geographies. Many people have sought to partake in the success of these corporations through the purchase of shares, or stock, in the company.

Ownership of company stock gives one the right of ownership of the company represented by the number of shares held. This ownership gives them the privilege available to owners of the company, again, to the extent of shares held. These are:

- Profiting from the upward price movements of the price of these shares, or experiencing losses when the price moves south.

- Earning dividends as and when declared.

- Voting on various decisions that require shareholder votes.

The ownership of stocks and trading in them has become very easy with the popularity of online brokerage accounts that can be opened with many providers. Most accounts will require purchases to be made against cash available in an account from where it can be collected by the brokerage for the purchase.

Experienced investors can get access to additional facilities like margin trading where they can trade against the value of existing holdings.

Investing in stocks directly gives the advantage of a direct benefit from upward price movements. At the same time, with a large number of stocks available, picking the right ones can be a challenge for most casual investors.

7.3.5 Bonds

A bond is a debt security. It is a loan given by the investor to the issuer of the bond. It comes with a fixed rate of interest as well as a defined maturity date. This rate is known as the "coupon rate." The rate offered could vary, based on the creditworthiness of the issuer. In line with the risk-reward principle discussed earlier, a less credible issuer may need to offer a higher rate to raise money, as compared to a more credible one, like the government.

Many investors favor bonds because they offer a fixed rate of return with the return of principle on maturity if the bonds are held to term, or till maturity. Many bond offerings, especially the ones of the government, come with tax benefits for investors.

Types of bonds

The three types of bonds, as defined by the U.S. Securities and Exchange Commission[21], in increasing order of risk, are:

U.S. Treasuries are issued by the U.S. Department of the Treasury on behalf of the federal government. They carry the full faith and credit of the US government, making them a safe and popular investment.

Municipal bonds, called "munis," are debt securities issued by states, cities, counties, and other government entities.

Corporate bonds are debt securities issued by private and public corporations.

Risk

Apart from the obvious credit risk of default by the borrower, bonds carry an interest rate risk.

If held to maturity, the bondholder will receive the full amount from a liquid issuer. However, if sold before maturity, the market value of the bonds is susceptible to change based on changes in the prevailing interest rates. In a rising interest rate environment, the demand for these bonds that pay a lower rate will be lower than newer bonds issued at higher rates.

---

21. What types of Bonds are there?," Bonds, Investor.gov, accessed on August 2, 2023, https://www.investor.gov/introduction-investing/investing-basics/investment-products/bonds-or-fixed-income-products/bonds

In order to transact, the price of the bond will need to be reduced so that the effective rate for a buyer becomes similar to prevailing rates.

Illustration:

Face value of bonds: $10,000
Tenure: 10 years
Coupon rate: 5% per annum
The bonds pay $500 to the investor every year.

Say, after 5 years, the interest rates have risen and new bonds, with the same credit risk rating, are being issued for a coupon rate of 7%.

What this means is that an investment of $10,000 will earn $700 every year.

In order to make the older bonds competitive, the current holder, if wishing to sell, will need to ensure that the $500 is paid by the bond translates to a 7% return. How can he do that?

$500 is 7% of what amount?
Or, $500/.07 = $7142.86

A buyer will be willing to buy these bonds, which have a face value of $10,000, for $7142.86. This is because the $500 per year which these bonds will continue to pay till maturity, now translates to a return of 7%, which is in line with prevailing market conditions.

Another risk present in bonds is "call risk." On occasion, the issuer could retire a bond before maturity, leading to the cessation of the income stream for the investor.

Quiz

1. **Which of the following aspects related to money could be said to be directly related to investing? (Select all applicable)**

   a. Acquisition

   b. Accumulation

   c. Preservation

   d. Growth

2. **In an inflationary world, prices tend to?**

   a. Rise

   b. Fall

   c. Stay unchanged

3. **In a world where prices fall over a period of time, in order to buy the same basket of goods and services as at the start of the period, we will need _____.**

   a. more money

   b. less money

   c. same amount of money

4. **No investment can be entirely risk-free.**

   a. Agree

   b. Disagree

5. **The FDIC compensates depositors of failed banks based on what criteria?**

   a. In the ratio of the money each depositor has in the failed bank

   b. Based on the amount of fees paid by the bank to FDIC

   c. A pre-determined limit per depositor

   d. First come first served basis

6. **Investment A promises a 4% return while Investment B promises a 6% return. Everything else being equal, which of the two is likely to be a riskier investment?**

   a. Investment A

   b. Investment B

   c. Not enough data to determine

7. **Which of the following could be considered riskier investments compared to listed stocks?**

   a. ETFs

   b. Bank CDs

   c. Corporate bonds

   d. None of the above

8. **The inability to access invested money when it is most needed is known as:**

    a. Interest rate risk

    b. Market risk

    c. Liquidity risk

    d. Sovereign risk

9. **Which of the following are ranged from low-risk to high-risk? You can select more than one.**

    a. Corporate Bond, Government Bond, Municipal Bond

    b. Municipal Bond, Government Bond, Corporate Bond

    c. Government Bond, Municipal Bond, Corporate Bond

    d. Municipal Bond, Corporate Bond, Government Bond

10. **Which of the following is the most diversified investment portfolio?**

    a. Equal investments in shares, bonds, CDs, and mutual funds

    b. Equal investments in shares of 4 different companies

    c. Equal investments in government bonds, municipal bonds, and corporate bonds

    d. Equal investments in 4 different ETFs

Answers	1 – c, d	2 – a	3 – b	4 – a	5 – c
	6 – b	7 – d	8 – c	9 – c	10 – a

Chapter Summary

◆ In this chapter we introduced the concept of investing.

◆ There is always some amount of risk inherent in investing.

◆ Risk and return generally trade off against each other.

◆ Diversification of one's portfolio is a fundamental, time-honored, investment strategy.

◆ Investment returns should be evaluated on a post-tax basis.

◆ Bank deposits, bonds, stocks, and mutual funds are today, the most popular choices for investment.

This page is intentionally left blank

Chapter **8**

Insurance

Insurance provides a safety net against the unexpected and undesirable events that can happen in life, such as a house being destroyed by fire, a car being stolen, a serious illness, or even an unexpected loss of life.

This chapter introduces the concept of insurance and the fundamentals based on which insurance contracts are issued.

It provides an overview of the major types of insurance which are:

- Life insurance

- Health insurance

- Motor insurance

- Home insurance

8.1 Introduction to Insurance

In its simplest form, insurance is the pooling of risk.

Unexpected events can happen in life. Though we keep trying to avert the possibility of being impacted by risks that unexpected events present, at one point in time or another, most of us suffer to some degree on account of them. They are a fact of life. Buildings catch fire, motor vehicles collide, and people get afflicted by serious ailments.

Insurance permits a large number of people to pay for creating a support system in the form of a pool of money that can be used to provide financial assistance to the few who do get impacted. Why, then, would a large number of people contribute to the pool?

Because the "who" cannot be predicted. Anyone who is at risk of possibly encountering a particular risk is a likely candidate to contribute to this pool, in order that he/she can draw from it if the need arises. Without being a contributor, the financial support of this pool would not be available.

But, why would someone buy your risk? Because the market is large enough for the risk to be diversified and reduced to a point where the purchaser, or insurer, is able to offset the cost of a few adverse incidents by many others who do not get impacted. This has evolved into a science through which risk is assessed and premium calculations made in order to ensure that the insurer does not end up with a loss. Further, through experience and knowledge, the cost of insurance is sought to be reduced through risk-reduction strategies.

8.2 Principles Underlying Insurance Contracts

8.2.1 Utmost good faith

The insured (policyholder) and the insurer are expected to act in good faith toward each other. This amounts to the insured providing relevant and truthful information that would enable the insurer to correctly evaluate the risk. It also requires the insurer to be transparent in the terms and conditions.

8.2.2 Insurable interest

Damage to the insured property or person could be expected to lead to financial loss.

8.2.3 Indemnity

The protection provided by the insurance is to restore the condition to what it was prior to the occurrence of the event that triggered the claim, to the extent provided for in the policy.

Compensation is designed to minimize loss, and not bestow riches. The insured is expected to act in a manner that promotes the minimization of risk.

8.2.4 Contribution

This enables the establishment of a corollary among all the insurance contracts related to the same incident.

What does it mean? If a piece of property is insured twice, it does not mean that the owner will be reimbursed twice in case of damage. It means that the total amount of reimbursement will remain the same but paid partially by both policies. Insurance is meant for reimbursement, not profit-making.

8.2.5 Subrogation

While compensating you for the loss from damage to an insured property, the insurer steps into the role of the owner of that property. This allows them to file for a claim from the party who may have been responsible for the damage for which they had to pay the insured.

This is limited to the amount paid to the insured. If they win back more, after accounting for expenses, the balance would need to be paid to the insured.

8.2.6 Proximate cause

It is difficult to define all possible causes that could cause damage. In case of damage, the cause that is primary to the event, or the most significant in triggering the event, needs to be established. If covered in the policy purchased, compensation is paid. Occasionally the proximate cause could be a reason for disputes as the insured and insurer may take different views.

8.3 Types of Insurance

There are many types of insurance that can be purchased. We may have heard of instances of actors insuring specific body parts against damage and singers insuring their voice and vocal cords in the same way.

However, for most people, the need for insurance will arise in only a few standard cases. These are what we will cover here.

8.3.1 Life insurance

Insuring one's life is a way of guaranteeing the continuance of the earning capability of the insured person in case of it being impaired by an event that leads to death or permanent damage or disability. The payout could be in the form of a lump sum or a recurring revenue stream. Life insurance is taken on the life of a person who is responsible for supporting others, the main purpose being to ensure that life for dependents can continue in a manner as close as possible to when the insured person was available.

Life insurance is considered to be an important part of the personal financial planning process for individuals and family units.

There are two main types of life insurance policies:

Term life

This is the purest form of life insurance. If death occurs while the policy is being serviced, a payout will be made. The day the policy stops, the benefit of payout upon death also ends.

Whole life

Whole life insurance is also known as permanent insurance. Premium is paid till death, at which point of time the death benefit is paid to the nominee or survivor. A whole life policy, unlike a term policy, also has a cash surrender value that can be received if the policy is canceled before death. Thus, it serves as an instrument of investment as well. This is why the premium for a whole life policy is much higher than for a term life policy.

8.3.2 Health insurance

Though designated as health insurance, and meant for the preservation of human health, in most cases it covers the medical expenses incurred by the insured for the preservation of health. Though health insurance is used interchangeably with "health cover" and "health benefits," in almost all cases the reference is to the protection being provided against the cost of medical services. And it is not a day too soon as healthcare and medical care costs have been rising rapidly in the US.

According to the Peterson-KFF Health System Tracker, the per capita expenditure on healthcare has gone up from $2,000 in 1970 to almost $13,000 in 2021, a six-fold jump in 50 years, measured in constant dollar terms of 2021.

| Figure 8.1 | Growth in national per capita health expenditure |

Total national health expenditures, US $ per capita, 1970-2021

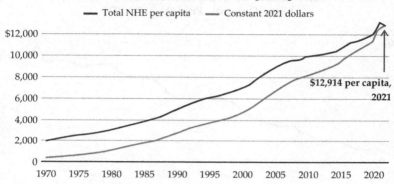

Note: A constant dollar is an inflation adjusted value used to compare dollar values from one period to another.

Source: KFF analysis of National Health Expenditure (NHE) data

Worryingly, healthcare spending has been going up faster than the GDP. It was a mere seven percent of the economy in 1970. It had reached 18.3 percent in 2021, excluding the blip of 19.7 percent in 2020 on account of higher health spending and lower GDP caused by the pandemic.

| Figure 8.2 | **Growth in health expenditure as a percentage of GDP** |

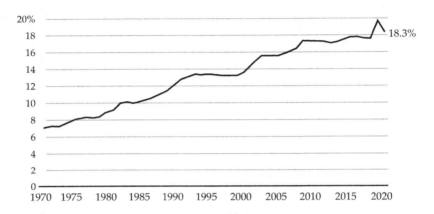

Total national health expenditures as a percent of
Gross Domestic Product, 1970-2021

Source: KFF analysis of National Health Expenditure (NHE) data

There is no running away from the burden of healthcare
expenses.

What is covered

A basic health insurance policy covers:

- Physician expenses – includes nonsurgical treatments and
  laboratory tests

- Surgical expenses – includes surgeon's fees and related
  expenses

- Hospital expenses – includes room and board expenses

Each of these will come with limits. The higher the limit, the
more expensive the policy will be.

In addition, this basic health insurance is often complemented by:

- Major medical insurance – this covers the expenses related to a serious injury or illness, that may quickly exhaust your basic policy limits.

- Dental insurance

- Vision insurance

Important terms in health insurance contracts

To understand the terms and conditions in a contract, it is important to understand these commonly used terms.

Deductible

The amount the insured pays before the insurer starts paying. A policy cover of $100,000 with a deductible of $2,000 means that the insurer comes into the picture only after the insured has paid the first $2,000. For expenses up to $2,000, the insurer pays nothing.

Co-pay

The responsibility to bear a certain portion of the cost, generally applicable to physician consultations and prescriptions. A $10 co-pay means that the insured will bear all expenses after the initial $10 has been paid. To illustrate, if your physician charges $40 for a consultation, you will pay $10 before the insurer pays the balance of $30.

Coinsurance

Shared payments of expenses by the insured and insurer on a percentage basis. Though conceptually similar to co-pay, as they both place partial responsibility for settling the payment on the insured, coinsurance is a percentage-based sharing of the cost while co-pay is a fixed-value payment.

Out-of-pocket expenses

Deductibles, co-pays, and coinsurance together constitute the out-of-pocket expenses. There could be an annual limit for these. If the total of the three has crossed the specified annual limit, the insurer will start picking up 100% of the remaining costs.

It must be remembered that though we would like the insurer to cover more/all expenses, taking on a part of the responsibility will have the effect of lowering the premium. Hence, they need to be considered. The industry also works on the assumption that making the insured responsible for the initial part of the expense reduces frivolous claims.

Insurance costs could vary from one insurer to another.

8.3.3 Motor insurance

If you own and drive a car, motor vehicle insurance is a requirement. Vehicle insurance and car insurance are other terms used for motor insurance.

The purpose of motor insurance is to protect you in case you incur a financial liability on account of your vehicle. It could be damage to the vehicle itself due to either the fault of others, like an errant driver hitting your car, or natural events for which a cause cannot be ascribed, such as a tree falling on your car. It can also protect you in case you are held responsible for damage to another person's vehicle and pay for the medical bills and repair costs of such others. Insurance can help you cover your legal costs as well in case of a suit for causing such an accident.

There could be some differences in motor insurance regulations between states, hence understanding the laws of the state where you usually drive will be helpful.

Types of cover

Liability

Covers you in case you are held responsible for causing damage to other vehicles and injury to other people. It is mandatory in most states.

Medical payment

This pays for the cost of injury to passengers of the vehicle, including yourself. A more comprehensive version of medical payment is the personal injury plan, which also covers the loss of wages, funeral costs, and other services that may be required as a result of the incident.

Collision coverage

This covers the damage to your vehicle. In case the car is totaled, or completely destroyed, it will also pay you the cash value equivalent of the car, since it is beyond repair.

Comprehensive

Since car damage is not always the result of crashes and collisions, comprehensive cover pays for losses and damages even in cases where the damage is on account of vandalism, theft, or natural causes.

Underinsured/uninsured motorist coverage

This cover is designed to protect you against other motorists who are irresponsible not from the perspective of poor driving, but driving without buying adequate insurance. In other words, the other driver is at fault but does not have the cover to pay for your damages and injuries.

Optional covers

Many auto insurance companies offer additional options that cover:

- Payment for a rental car while the insured car is being repaired.

- Roadside assistance in case you are stranded.

- Gap insurance to pay off the balance outstanding on the car loan, in the specific case the car is totaled and the cash equivalent does not cover it fully. You still have the loan for the car but no car.

Fun fact;

Since consumers can choose the cover they want and how much, each policy can be different. The cover is generally expressed as *xx/yy/zz* where:

xx is the amount the policy will pay for the medical expenses of each individual

yy is the total amount to be paid for medical expenses

zz is the cover for the property damaged, whether another person's car or some other object

Factors affecting car insurance pricing

Several factors are taken into account by insurers for determining the premium. A lower premium can be expected for the following reasons:

- Good driving history, with fewer, or none, accidents
- Lower expected use of the vehicle, such as people working from home
- Location in less dense or lower crime-rate neighborhoods
- Higher age, typically equating to longer driving experience
- Gender – in several gender and age combinations, female drivers have better-driving statistics and pay lower premiums.
- Vehicles identified as being easy and less costly to maintain and repair

- Good credit score – some states have banned using credit score as criteria for premium calculation

- Vehicles that have enhanced security features installed, such as anti-theft devices, anti-lock brakes, etc.

- Overall relationship with the insurer - if you have multiple cars insured with the same company

8.3.4 Home insurance

This is a form of property insurance that pertains to private property, It is also referred to as homeowners' insurance.

A home is the most expensive or valuable possession of most individuals. The value of the owned property often is the biggest contributor to the wealth of an individual. It, therefore, makes sense to ensure that the property is kept safe from any form of deterioration in value. This is done through regular upkeep and maintenance of the property as well as taking out insurance as a form of protection against unforeseen events.

What is covered?

While most policies seek to provide cover against unforeseen events, there are some standard inclusions in home insurance policies:

Structure

This is the physical structure of your home, which can be repaired or rebuilt in the event of damage or destruction from events listed in the policy. Detached structures such as garages and tool sheds are also covered, generally for a small additional premium. Covers against earthquakes and floods are generally not included. Hence, if living in areas prone to these events, they must be added on.

A rule of thumb is to buy insurance for an amount that will enable you to rebuild the home ground up.

Personal belongings

A home is a home because it houses people as well as the things that are important to those people. Just as a house structure can be damaged or destroyed, so can the articles inside the structure.

Personal belongings are covered by home insurance policies, generally for values lower than the structure. It is a good idea to do an inventory of the belongings, especially of the expensive items like jewelry, art, and silverware, in order that adequate cover can be ensured. Interestingly, home policies also cover off-premises stored items. It means that an item that was stolen from your hotel room when on travel, could also be covered in the same policy.

Property and items belonging to others are not covered unless specifically listed as additional insured items. In some cases, the policy could offer limited coverage for the personal property of tenants and guests.

Liability protection

This protects you against claims in case you, or others, like children and pets, who are your responsibility, destroy the property of others. Once again, your home is intact and damage-free, but some property outside the home has been damaged. This cover protects you against such events. In much the same way, if an outsider is injured inside your premises, say, by a falling tree branch, this cover will pay for the medical bills of treatment for the injured person. This also covers the cost of the defense in case there is a legal case filed. Unfortunately, if your pets destroy your expensive Persian rug, this protection may not be available to you.

Living expenses

If the property becomes unusable as a result of the incident, and you are forced to rent another property, or live in a hotel for a bit, and incur expenses on food and travel, these expenses are covered for the period the home is unusable.

Again, these are not carte blanche allowances but have limits prescribed either in dollar terms or in terms of a period. Even rent foregone can be covered.

Special types of home insurance

In general, home insurance refers to homeowner's insurance. However, there are some specific types that are different.

Renter's insurance

Even if you are not the owner, you can still insure your possessions through a home insurance policy, while the landlord might be insuring the structure of what you have rented from him.

Condominium and co-op insurance

The structure of policies that cover condominiums and co-op apartments is a little different since there is shared ownership of the structure.

The coverage structure for these units is through a combination of two policies:

1. Master policy for the structure that is taken out by the society or association

2. Individual policy that covers the owner's belongings as well as any specific items of the structure of the apartment not covered by the master policy

Against what risks does a homeowner's insurance provide cover?

Home insurance operates on the basis of coverage of "named perils." Anything that is not named is not covered. An "open perils" policy is one that covers everything except the perils specifically named as not covered. There are multiple levels of "named peril" coverage. The basic level covers a few obvious ones like fire, lightning, and windstorm. Obviously, the premium increases with the expansion of coverage.

Perils excluded:

- Earthquake

- Flood

- Power failure

- War

- Nuclear hazard

- Neglect

- Intentional act

- Ordinance of law

8.4 Pricing of Insurance

Considering that insurance is protection against future events, how does one price it, considering that future events cannot be predicted?

In general, the higher the risk, the higher the premium. Insurance companies rely on past data and superimpose it with their view of the future to arrive at the probability of an event happening in the future.

Illustration:

Let us say that there are 1,000 cars in a particular community served by a single insurance cooperative insurance company (no profit no loss) that insures all 1,000 cars.

According to past data, the insurance company knows that every year they pay out $500,000 as motor insurance claims, due to various causes, to 50 claimants.

Now, to support a payout of $500,000, they need to collect that amount from the insured vehicle owners as a premium.

Collecting $500,000 from 1,000 owners means that they collect $500 as a premium from each of the 1,000 owners.

But, this is a simplistic illustration. In the real world, adjustments need to be made for complexities such as:

The insurance company also has staff and systems that they use for handling this work. They need to pay for that as well.

Each car and each owner is different and presents a different risk of a claim. An adjustment has to be made for that. It is not fair for safe drivers to pay as much premium as rash drivers.

Other companies could be vying for the same customers, making pricing more competitive.

8.4.1 Actuarial life table

In this context, a mention needs to be made of actuarial life tables that calculate and depict the probability of a person of a specific age dying in the next 12 months. They are useful for decisions that are based on mortality rates in the future, hence are of vital importance to insurance companies who price their risk based on these tables.

Actuarial rates are expected to indicate the most competitive premium that should be charged and expressed in terms of units of exposure.

Table 8.1	Sample actuarial table

Age (years)	Probability of dying between ages x and $x+1$	Number surviving to age x	Number dying between ages x and $x+1$	Person-years lived between ages x and $x+1$	Total number of person-years lived above age x	Expectation of life at age x
	q_x	l_x	d_x	L_x	T_x	e_x
0-1	0.005864	100,000	586	99,487	7,865,195	78.7
1-2	0.000396	99,414	39	99,394	7,765,707	78.1
2-3	0.000262	99,374	26	99,361	7,666,314	77.1
3-4	0.000197	99,348	20	99,338	7,566,952	76.2
4-5	0.000158	99,329	16	99,321	7,467,614	75.2
5-6	0.000151	99,313	15	99,305	7,368,293	74.2
6-7	0.000135	99,298	13	99,291	7,268,988	73.2
7-8	0.000121	99,285	12	99,279	7,169,697	72.2
8-9	0.000108	99,273	11	99,267	7,070,418	71.2
9-10	0.000095	99,262	9	99,257	6,971,151	70.2
10-11	0.000089	99,252	9	99,248	6,871,894	69.2
11-12	0.000095	99,244	9	99,239	6,772,646	68.2
12-13	0.000122	99,234	12	99,228	6,673,407	67.2
13-14	0.000175	99,222	17	99,213	6,574,179	66.3
14-15	0.000249	99,205	25	99,192	6,474,965	65.3
15-16	0.000328	99,180	33	99,164	6,375,773	64.3
16-17	0.000410	99,147	41	99,127	6,276,609	63.3
17-18	0.000502	99,107	50	99,082	6,177,482	62.3
18-19	0.000603	99,057	60	99,027	6,078,400	61.4
19-20	0.000706	98,997	70	98,962	6,979,373	60.4
20-21	0.000814	98,927	80	98,887	5,880,411	59.4
21-22	0.000914	98,847	90	98,802	5,781,524	58.5
22-23	0.000994	98,757	98	98,707	5,682,722	57.5
23-24	0.001048	98,658	103	98,607	5,584,014	56.6
24-25	0.001083	98,555	107	98,502	5,485,408	55.7
25-26	0.001112	98,448	109	98,394	5,386,906	54.7
26-27	0.001143	98,339	112	98,283	5,288,512	53.8
27-28	0.001177	98,226	116	98,169	5,190,230	52.8
28-29	0.001216	98,111	119	98,051	5,092,061	51.9
29-30	0.001260	97,992	123	97,930	4,994,010	51.0

Age (years)	Probability of dying between ages x and $x+1$	Number surviving to age x	Number dying between ages x and $x+1$	Person-years lived between ages x and $x+1$	Total number of person-years lived above age x	Expectation of life at age x
	q_x	l_x	d_x	L_x	T_x	e_x
30-31	0.001306	97,868	128	97,804	4,896,080	50.0
31-32	0.001353	97,740	132	97,674	4,798,276	49.1
32-33	0.001401	97,608	137	97,540	4,700,602	48.2
33-34	0.001451	97,471	141	97,401	4,603,062	47.2
34-35	0.001504	97,330	146	97,257	4,505,662	46.3
35-36	0.001566	97,183	152	97,107	4,408,405	45.4
36-37	0.001635	97,031	159	96,952	4,311,298	44.4
37-38	0.001701	96,873	163	96,790	4,214,346	43.5
38-39	0.001763	96,708	170	96,623	4,117,555	42.6
39-40	0.001827	96,537	176	96,449	4,020,933	41.7
40-41	0.001907	96,361	184	96,269	3,924,484	40.7
41-42	0.002011	96,177	193	96,080	3,828,214	39.8
42-43	0.002136	95,984	205	95,881	3,732,134	38.9
43-44	0.002280	95,779	218	95,670	3,636,253	38.0
44-45	0.002445	95,560	234	95,444	3,540,583	37.1
45-46	0.002621	95,327	250	95,202	3,445,139	36.1
46-47	0.002821	95,077	268	94,943	3,349,938	35.2
47-48	0.003066	94,809	291	94,663	3,254,995	34.3
48-49	0.003369	94,518	318	94,359	3,160,331	33.4
49-50	0.003720	94,200	350	94,025	3,065,972	32.5
50-51	0.004090	93,849	384	93,657	2,971,948	31.7
51-52	0.004474	93,465	418	93,256	2,878,291	30.8
52-53	0.004891	93,047	455	92,820	2,786,034	29.9
53-54	0.005344	92,592	495	92,345	2,692,214	29.1
54-55	0.005822	92,097	536	91,829	2,599,870	28.2
55-56	0.006319	91,561	579	91,272	2,508,040	27.4
56-57	0.006825	90,983	621	90,672	2,416,768	26.6
57-58	0.007341	90,362	663	90,030	2,326,095	25.7
58-59	0.007877	89,698	707	89,345	2,236,066	24.9
59-60	0.008447	88,992	752	88,616	2,146,721	24.1
60-61	0.009065	88,240	800	87,840	2,058,106	23.3

Quiz

1. **In its simplest form, insurance can be called the:**

   a. Separation of risk

   b. Pooling of risk

   c. Measurement of risk

   d. Quantification of risk

2. **In insurance, a few people contribute to create a pool of money that is then used to defray the financial cost of unforeseen events on a larger number of people.**

   a. Agree

   b. Disagree

3. **Insurance seeks to compensate for losses arising from the impact of? (Select all applicable)**

   a. Events that are uncertain

   b. Events that are certain

   c. Events in the past

   d. Events in the future

4. **The universe of people who can seek support from the insurance pool are: (Select all applicable)**

   a. The ones who have been adversely impacted by the same event in the past

   b. The ones living in the same area as the head office of the insurance company

   c. The ones who have contributed to it

   d. The ones who have not taken money from the pool in the past

5. **The money paid by the insured people to create the pool used to support people suffering losses is known as:**

   a. Contribution

   b. Annuity

   c. Interest

   d. Premium

6. **The insured can insure _____.**

   a. any property

   b. only property belonging to him/her

   c. only property that does not belong to him/her

   d. None of the above

7. **Indemnification for losses incurred is _____.**

   a. limited to the extent provided in the policy

   b. limited to the extent of money required to restore to pre-damage state

   c. lower of a and b

   d. higher of a and b

8. **In case the insured has taken multiple covers from several insurance companies for the same property, in case of damage, the overriding principle is that he can _____.**

   a. only claim from one company

   b. claim from all separately

   c. claim towards indemnification of losses and costs

   d. not make any claim as all claims become void since he insured multiple times

9. **The proximate cause is _____.**

   a. one of the causes of damage for which protection has been sought

   b. the exact cause responsible for the damage

   c. the cause primarily responsible for the event

   d. the list of all possible causes for which cover can be bought

10. Everything else being equal, the life insurance premium paid by a person, in comparison to what is paid by a person 10 years younger, will be:

a. Lower

b. Higher

c. Same

Answers	1 – b	2 – b	3 – a, d	4 – c	5 – d
	6 – b	7 – c	8 – c	9 – c	10 – b

Chapter Summary

◆ In its simplest form insurance is the pooling of risk. It permits a large number of people to pay for creating a support system in the form of a pool of money that can be used to provide financial assistance to the few who do get impacted by unexpected events.

◆ The principles that underlie a contract of insurance are indemnification, utmost good faith, insurable interest, contribution, subrogation, and proximate cause.

◆ The four main types of insurance that individuals opt for are life insurance, health insurance, motor insurance, and home insurance.

◆ Each of these types of insurance could have several policy subtypes as well as types of cover associated with them.

◆ Pricing of insurance is an effort at pricing the risk associated with the event insured. In general, the higher the risk, the higher the premium.

Chapter 9

Taxation

Governments need money to fund the promises they make to their constituents and the services the constituents expect from them.

Taxation is the source of revenue for governments. They levy taxes, of different types, in order to fund their operations. Even though in democratic societies the government is a representative of the people, invariably, efforts at levying or raising taxation are met with resistance and cynicism from the taxed.

This chapter makes a case for why taxation is required and creates awareness about the various types of taxes. This chapter also:

- discusses income tax rates

- provides an overview of the income tax filing process

- discusses general guidelines and principles around taxation

9.1 The Case for Taxation

From the individual's perspective, taxation takes away a part of the fruit of his/her labor.

From the government's perspective, taxation enables them to create an environment where the population can ply their trade and earn money.

The tax code reflects the thinking of the society where it applies and keeps getting updated as societal thinking evolves. As a result, at times, the taxation structure appears to be unwieldy and complex, which requires expertise to navigate. However, in most civil societies, there is a logic behind most changes in the tax code.

The government in the US operates at three levels – federal, state, and municipal. All three have the right to impose taxes according to the areas within their jurisdiction. Some areas, like income tax, cut across the governance boundaries and can be used by all three government layers. This can cause confusion for the taxpayer. Similar confusion can also arise for people with international income and mobility and raise questions like "Should tax be paid where they live or where they earn?"

Of course, as issues arise and become common, governments do make an effort to address them for the future.

9.2 Income Tax

Income tax is the most commonly used method of taxation.

Almost everyone has a means of earning income with which they meet their expenses. This enables income tax to be applicable to a large part of the population.

The US tax code is based on the idea that everyone should help finance the government according to one's ability to pay, taxing income in a progressive manner, the tax rates progressively become higher as your income increases, enabling the administration to adhere to this principle. The tax rates are also known as tax brackets or tax slabs. It is also expected that the higher earners should be willing to pay more because they have received greater benefits from the system in the form of higher earnings.

9.2.1 Income tax rates

The IRS publishes the tax rates applicable. The latest rates available at the time of going to press are for the tax year 2023, which are produced below:

- 37% for incomes over $578,125 ($693,750 for married couples filing jointly)

- 35% for incomes over $231,250 ($462,500 for married couples filing jointly)

- 32% for incomes over $182,100 ($364,200 for married couples filing jointly)

- 24% for incomes over $95,375 ($190,750 for married couples filing jointly)

- 22% for incomes over $44,725 ($89,450 for married couples filing jointly)

- 12% for incomes over $11,000 ($22,000 for married couples filing jointly)

- 10% for incomes under $11,000 ($22,000 for married couples filing jointly)

Married people filing separately follow individual brackets. The head of household gets a certain additional allowance, with tier limits being higher.

9.2.2 US federal income tax process

Who should file

The IRS specifies the minimum income criteria for filing federal income tax returns. For example, if you are single, and under 65 on the last day of 2022, you need to file if your income exceeds $12,950 and $14,700 if you are 65 or older.

Even if filing is not mandatory based on income, filing a return is recommended. It can help you get your money back or receive credits in several situations.

When to file

Individuals are expected to file tax returns on a calendar year basis. For income during the year 2022, the IRS has specified April 18, 2023, as the last date for returns to be filed.

How to file

Income tax returns can be filed either electronically or sent through regular mail. The IRS encourages e-filing. E-filed returns are eligible for faster refunds. Form 1040 is the prescribed form for individual tax returns.

9.2.3 General principles

Income tax is mainly a federal prerogative but many states and municipalities also levy income tax. These taxes paid to non-federal entities can be taken as credits for the calculation of federal taxes.

Income tax is levied on the global income of eligible people. If the same income has been taxed in an overseas jurisdiction, double taxation avoidance agreements allow for it to not be taxed a second time.

Certain individual expenses can be used to set off income, notably mortgage interest, local and state taxes, and contributions to charities.

The principle of marginality applies to income tax. What this means is that the higher rate of tax in the next higher slab is only applicable to the extent to which income exceeds the limit of the previous tier.

9.3 Other Major Taxes

9.3.1 Sales tax

This is a tax levied on the basis of consumption. You pay for a product and the applicable sales tax when you buy it. It is also known as consumption tax. Sales tax is seen as a fair method of taxation because consumption reflects means and income. Moreover, only people who buy a certain product pay for it.

Opponents of sales tax argue that people with lower incomes spend a greater percentage of it on consumption and, consequently, on sales tax, since the tax on a product does not differentiate between income levels of purchasers.

State and local governments levy sales tax in the US. Many jurisdictions outside the US are moving on to the concept of a goods and services tax (GST) which is similar to sales tax, but where the value added at each stage of the supply chain is taxed.

9.3.2 Excise taxes

Excise duties are typically levied on items of a discretionary nature, as opposed to necessities like food and electricity. Items like cigarettes and alcohol are the types of consumptive spends likely to attract excise.

The logic for excise seems to emanate from the need to control behavior through the taxation of some items. In a way, the government seeks to give out a message saying, "We think cigarettes are bad, but if you still must consume them, pay more for it." Opponents of excise harp on this "social engineering" goal as a criticism. Some people refer to it as "sin tax."

9.3.3 Property tax

Property tax seeks to tax property holdings, not merely land and buildings but also items of high value such as cars and boats. It is also sometimes known as wealth tax.

Items taxed usually are ones that hold significant value and reflect the principle of taxing based on ability to pay. Items taxed are usually the ones where reasonable records of holding are available in the form of deeds and licenses.

9.3.4 Estate taxes

Also known as inheritance tax, these are levied on the transfer of property from the deceased to the living. Opponents of estate taxes cite this as an example of double taxation since the income, based on which the wealth was created, would already have been taxed when earned.

9.3.5 Customs duty

This is a tax imposed on the importation of certain goods. The objective usually is to protect goods of a similar kind being produced locally, by making it more expensive to buy goods not made locally.

9.3.6 Capital gains tax

Federal income tax is imposed on capital gains. Capital gains refer to gains on the sale of certain assets, such as property and shares. While short-term holding, of less than a year, leads to taxation at the rate at which the individual is assessed to income tax, longer-term holding attracts lower rates of taxation.

9.3.7 Payroll tax

This is actually a basket of taxes and covers contributions to government programs such as medicare, social security, unemployment, disability, and others.

Quiz

---

1. **The primary purpose of taxation is _____.**

   a. to keep the people in check

   b. to fund government schemes and services

   c. to check the wealth of each individual

   d. None of the above

2. **The major source of revenue for a government is:**

   a. Taxes

   b. Utility payments

   c. Selling arms and ammunition

   d. None of the above

3. **Individuals would like to pay _____.**

   a. higher taxes

   b. lower taxes

4. **Income tax in the US can be collected by _____.**

   a. only the federal government

   b. only the state governments

   c. only the municipal governments

   d. all three governments

5. **The reason income tax is popular with most governments is:**

    a. It is the easiest to administer

    b. It yields the highest revenue for the government

    c. Almost everyone has some income and hence is eligible for income tax assessment

    d. It is the most transparent

6. **One of the underlying principles of the US tax code is:**

    a. Everyone should finance the government in direct proportion to earnings.

    b. Everyone should finance the government according to their ability to pay.

    c. Everyone should finance the government equally, regardless of income.

7. **Progressive taxation means: (Select all applicable)**

    a. Income tax rates increase as income increases

    b. Income tax rates decrease as income increases

    c. Income tax rates increase as income decreases

    d. Income tax rates decrease as income decreases

8. **For married people filing taxes jointly, the slab lower levels, when compared to individuals, are:**

   a. Higher

   b. Lower

   c. Same

9. **The slab levels for filing income tax returns as the head of the household are:**

   a. The same as for individual filers

   b. The same as for married couples filing jointly

   c. The same as for married couples filing individually

   d. Different from all of the above

10. **The income taxed is:**

   a. Income earned in the US

   b. Income earned globally

Answers	1 – b	2 – a	3 – b	4 – d	5 – c
	6 – b	7 – a, d	8 – a	9 – d	10 – b

Chapter Summary

◆ In this chapter we introduced the concept of taxation for individuals and the need for it.

◆ There are several types of taxes that are applicable. The most common ones are income tax, sales tax, excise, property tax, estate duty, capital gains tax, and Payroll tax.

◆ The US federal income tax process defines who needs to file tax returns, by what date, and the rates that are applicable.

Chapter **10**

Retirement Planning

While the natural process of aging has always existed, the formal process of retirement and the planning around it could be said to be under a hundred years old, around the time when the concept of social security was introduced. This coincided with the rapid growth of consumer businesses as well as the development of financial markets, creating many options for individuals to invest and earn from.

In effect, the process requires one to save money during the time of life when one is active and able, with the starting and ending points being generally between the ages of 25 and 65 for most people and then investing the savings in a manner that one can live off them during the sunset years when one is not able to earn.

It discusses:

- Historical perspective on retirement
- Linkage of retirement and life expectancy

- The sources of retirement security

- Estate planning and creating a will

- Planning for retirement

10.1 Historical Perspective On Retirement

A number of changes were introduced in the financial environment in the aftermath of the Great Depression of the early thirties. One of them was the introduction of social security. The introduction of social security brought an official ring to the "before and after" concept of active years and retired years.

While there is no defined date for retirement, 66 is generally considered to be the age at which retirement begins, since one becomes eligible for social security drawdowns around that time. Most age classifications of official data also have a 65, or 66 and over age bracket.

The traditional concept of retirement required one to keep putting away a part of the income during one's working years to build up a corpus. This would be used during the golden years when one either could not or did not want to pursue active work. Instead, the focus would be on all the things that one wanted to do but could not do during the working years.

10.2 Retirement and Life Expectancy

There has been a steady increase in life expectancy in the US. The chart below is based on data made available by Our World in Data and shows that life expectancy at birth has gone up from under 50 in 1901 to 79 in 2020, dipping again in 2021, hopefully temporarily.

Figure 10.1 **Movement in life expectancy at birth in the US**

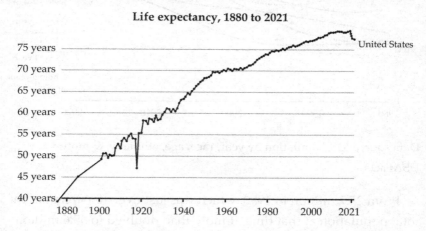

Life expectancy, 1880 to 2021

Note: Shown is the 'period life expectancy'. This is the average number of years a newborn would live if age-specific mortality rates in the current year were to stay the same throughout its life.

Source: Our World in Data (Life Expectancy - Our World in Data)

Life expectancy at birth refers to the average age a child born in that year could hope to live to. A life expectancy of 50 in the year 1902 means that children born in that year would live to an average age of 50. So, it's good, isn't it, that we are living longer?

Sure, but there are implications of living longer that we need to understand. Like retirement. According to USAFacts, the fastest-growing population segment by age has been the over-65 cohort.

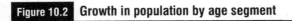

Figure 10.2 **Growth in population by age segment**

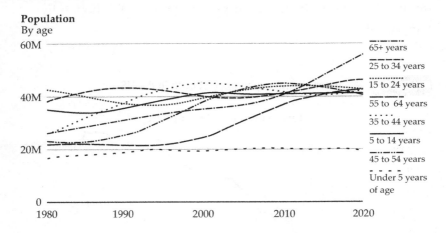

Data source: US population by year, race, age, ethnicity, & more | USAFacts

From 25.7 million in 1980, which was just over 10 percent of the total population at that time, it more than doubled to 55.6 million in 2022 and reached close to 17 percent of the total population of 333 million.

It is great that people are living longer. But the issue is, longer life and lifestyle need to be supported and paid for. You still need to eat. You still need a home. You still need to pay for health and medical expenses. And, in most cases, you need to pay for it yourself, while you can. Create a corpus that you can draw from. To support a longer post-retirement life you need to save more during the working years.

Till 1944, the probability of the retired adult enjoying the fruits of his savings was low, since the average person did not live beyond 65. Even in 1964, with a life expectancy of 70, only 5 years of post-retirement expenses were needed by most people. However, the requirement has kept increasing, along with which has gone up the need to save a larger part of earnings during working years.

Illustration:

Let us assume the working years are 26 through 65, with retirement at 66, considered as the full retirement age for social security payments.

Life expectancy crossed 65 in 1944.

Over 40 years, from age 26 through 65, if a person earns $50,000 a year and spends $40,000, his savings will amount to $10,000, all in current dollar equivalent value. The savings will accumulate to $400,000 over 40 years, represented by the trend line below.

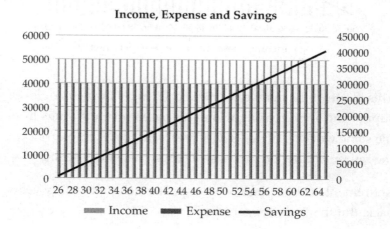

The person is 65 years old in the last year shown on the chart and retires.

If we are in 1940, with a life expectancy under 65 years, there is not much use for the money saved for retirement. It will pass on as per law.

Post 1964, when life expectancy reached 70, the average person has 5 years to live after retirement. If he continues to maintain the same lifestyle and spends $40,000 a year in retirement, he will start drawing from the accumulated $400,000 but will still have $200,000 left over at the time he passes.

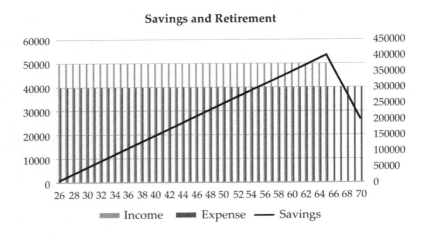

Savings and Retirement

This is one of the main retirement challenges facing people. Of supporting an increasingly long life based on the savings from the same working life of, say, 40 years. In this example, once the retirement period exceeds 10 years, challenges begin.

Retirement is not a place people spent much time in fifty years back. But that is no longer true.

10.3 The Sources of Retirement Security

Traditionally, retirees have relied upon the "three-legged stool" of retirement income. It consists of:

10.3.1 Social security

The largest federal government program in the US, social security provides retirement, as well as disability and survivor benefits to eligible individuals. Workers contribute to it during their working years and draw from it upon retirement.

10.3.2 Pension

Also known as a defined benefit plan, these are run by employers and usually guarantee an income after retirement based on the size of the pot that has been created.

Defined benefit plans are increasingly being replaced by defined contribution plans that are contributed to by the employee and sometimes by the employer, but do not guarantee a return. The return is based on the investment choices made by the contributor and the amount invested. 401(k)s, 403(b)s and 457(b) s – are the best-known defined contribution plans.

401(k)

This is the most commonly used plan amongst all types and sizes of employers. An employee can contribute with pre-tax wages; he/she does not have to pay tax on the amount contributed out of salary. Retirement withdrawals are subject to applicable tax. Early withdrawal may attract additional taxes.

403(b)

This one is similar to 401(k) but is meant for public school employees and employees of some organizations that are exempt from tax.

457(b)

This plan is available to employees of state and local governments.

10.3.3 Personal savings

Personal savings can come in many forms and usually lead to the building of assets during one's working life which yields returns, or income, during the retirement phase. Rental from property and dividends from stocks are examples of such savings.

The government, in a bid to support retirement planning, also chips in with incentives for certain accounts, usually through tax benefits. There are other types of plans that can be taken up by individuals without the need for an employer to be involved. These are useful for self-employed people who are both employers and employees.

Popular choices available:

Traditional IRA (Individual Retirement Account)

Originally meant for people not covered by employer insurance, they were later made available to everyone. They can be funded through tax-deductible contributions (up to defined limits) as well as non-deductible ones. The funds can be invested in a wide range of financial products such as stocks, bonds, mutual funds, and CDs.

Roth IRA

This was introduced in 1997. Contributions are not tax deductible, but withdrawals are not taxed either. You can have both a traditional IRA as well as a ROTH IRA at the same point, with contributions being subject to defined limits. Capital appreciation in IRA accounts is not taxed.

Guaranteed income annuity

This is a way of creating a defined benefit on your own. By investing a certain amount in the plan, individuals guarantee themselves a pension for life based on the provider's plan. They can invest a bulk amount or do the same over a period of time.

Cash-value life insurance

This is a type of life insurance plan which builds up a corpus over a period of time while offering death benefits from the time the plan is purchased. The cash value serves to fulfill a part of retirement financial needs.

10.4 Estate Planning and Creating a Will

Everything you own is a part of your estate. Despite life expectancy going up, the uncertainty of life continues. While in general people may be living longer, some individuals will not;

nobody really knows when that will be. Hence, it is a good idea to plan for that eventuality.

Estate planning helps you put your affairs in a state where they can be managed according to your wishes, even after your death. By doing so, you are making it easier for your successors and loved ones.

A will is the written instruction of a deceased person, created obviously before death, regarding the disposal of his/her estate, or belongings. The distribution of assets is carried out after the liabilities and debts of the deceased have been settled. The deceased cannot transfer merely his assets and leave the liabilities unaddressed.

Any mentally competent adult can write a will. It needs to be witnessed by at least two people who are not beneficiaries. It can be written afresh at any later time, making the previous will redundant.

Estate taxes are applicable on the estate that is marked for distribution. One of the objectives of estate planning is also to effectively manage this aspect.

General recommendations for a will:

- An executor should be named who will be responsible for discharging debts and distributing the funds as per the mandate.

- A new will should be drawn up when your life situation changes significantly. Events like marriage, divorce, and childbirth, could be considered significant. Even an existing beneficiary's death should create the need for a new will. Also significant would be a material change in circumstances, for the better or for the worse.

- Instructions for your care at a time when you are not in a position to manage your health and care. A loved one could be appointed as a power of attorney with specific authorities. This is also known as a "living will." It would also designate a healthcare proxy, a person to take decisions regarding your treatment, including end-of-life wishes.

- Estate taxes diminish the value of your estate that will be distributed to your beneficiaries. For that reason, one of the purposes of estate planning is to try to minimize those taxes.

10.5 Planning for Retirement

Retirement security does not happen on its own. One has to work towards it.

Considering its importance for an age-group cohort that could be vulnerable, not only does the government introduce savings plans from time to time geared towards retirement, but also its agencies regularly issue guidelines on navigating the retirement period.

The United States Department of Labor[22] has issued a handy 10-point guideline, the key points of which are:

- The earlier one starts saving the better

---

22. "Top 10 Ways to Prepare for Retirement," Employee Benefits Security Administration, United States Department of Labor, September 2021, https://www.dol.gov/sites/dolgov/files/ebsa/about-ebsa/our-activities/resource-center/publications/top-10-ways-to-prepare-for-retirement.pdf

- The more one saves the better

- Follow basic investment principles for the money you are saving

- One should familiarize himself/herself with the available options

- Project your financial needs in retirement

- Open an IRA account

- Don't touch your retirement savings

- Ask your employer to start a retirement plan if they do not already offer one

- Know the implications of early and late withdrawal of social security

- Make an effort to inform yourself

Quiz

1. **Social security was introduced in the US:**

   a. After independence

   b. After the Civil War

   c. After the Great Depression

   d. Before the first World War

2. **The eligibility for social security drawdowns begins:**

   a. After 58

   b. After 60

   c. After 65

   d. After 75

3. **Life expectancy at birth in the US has been:**

   a. Increasing

   b. Decreasing

   c. Constant

4. **As a result of increasing life expectancy, people are spending:**

   a. Fewer years in retirement

   b. More years in retirement

5. **If the years spent in retirement decrease, _____.**

   a. people will need to save less money for retirement

   b. people will need to save more money for retirement

6. **The "three-legged" stool of retirement income consists of:**

   a. Social security, stocks, and bonds

   b. Pension, bonds, and CDs

   c. CDs, pension, and traditional IRA account

   d. Social security, pension, and personal savings

7. **Pension plans that guarantee income after retirement are known as:**

   a. Defined benefit plans

   b. Defined contribution plans

8. **Social security contributions come from:**

   a. The covered workers

   b. The government

   c. The employer

   d. All of the above

9. **Select the statements that are true.**

   a. Defined contribution plans are increasingly being replaced by defined benefit plans.

   b. Defined benefit plans are increasingly being replaced by defined contribution plans.

   c. There is no significant change in composition between defined benefit and defined contribution plans.

10. **Select all true statements.**

    a. In defined contribution plans, the retirement income responsibility is on the employer.

    b. In defined contribution plans, the retirement income responsibility is on the employee.

    c. In defined benefit plans, the retirement income responsibility is on the employer.

    d. In defined benefit plans, the retirement income responsibility is on the employee.

Answers	1 – c	2 – c	3 – a	4 – b	5 – a
	6 – d	7 – a	8 – a	9 – b	10 – b, c

Chapter Summary

◆ This chapter introduced retirement, the need to save for retirement and the various ways in which it can be done.

◆ Retirement, as a formal process, seems to owe its birth to the introduction of social security, in the aftermath of The Great Depression.

◆ With life expectancy increasing, the pressure to save more for longer years of retirement has been increasing.

◆ Retirees have traditionally relied upon the "three-legged stool" for sustenance during their later years. The three-legged stool comprises pension, personal savings, and social security.

◆ Estate planning and the creation of a will are recommended activities for all retirees that are designed to ensure a smooth, hassle-free transition to the successor/s.

◆ The United States Department of Labor has issued a handy 10-point guideline to guide and inform the retirement planning process.

Made in United States
Orlando, FL
22 June 2024